WSKids
WHITE STAR KIDS

CODING
FOR
KIDS

CREATE YOUR OWN
VIDEOGAMES
WITH SCRATCH

SCRATCH PROJECTS BY **CODER KIDS**

ILLUSTRATIONS BY VALENTINA FIGUS

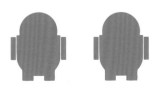

SCRATCH 2.0

VARIABLES
STAGE **OBJECT**
MOVEMENT **SPRITE**
PROJECTS
CLICK
LOOP LEVELS **DIRECTION**
RANDOM NUMBER
FOREVER
BACKDROP ARROW **CLICK**

CONTENTS

PAGE 4   Why Learn Programming?

PAGE 8   Scratch 2.0

PAGE 10   Sprites, Stages, Scripts

PAGE 12   Areas

PAGE 13   Tools

PAGE 14   Blocks

PAGE 17   Panes

PAGE 18   Projects

PAGE 21   Smash the Mosquito

PAGE 33   The Racetrack

PAGE 47   Catch me if you can!

PAGE 61   Everybody to the Seaside

PAGE 79   The Crazy Umbrella

PAGE 97   Jellyfish Salad

PAGE 118   Solutions

PAGE 127   Acknowledgments

Why Learn Programming?

"Don't just buy a new video game, make one. Don't just download the latest app, help design it. Don't just play on your phone, program it."

Barack Obama

In the early years of the new millennium the concept of computational thinking made a lot of headway in the discussion about the new frontiers in education. The term does not refer to the ability to use a computer as a tool, but rather to the mental ability needed to conceptualize problems so as to use machines to solve them.

It is becoming more and more widely accepted that this ability ought to be promoted alongside language and basic math skills in elementary schools.

This series is designed to introduce kids to the basic concepts of programming. Using a language created especially for them (Scratch 2.0), young readers can learn to code and create games that get increasingly complex. But the aim is not to train young programmers: by introducing them to programming the book seeks to teach children to express their creativity with a new tool, to find new, original and effective solutions to problems, and above all to allow them to see the beauty and the possibility of creating their own projects and realizing their own ideas from scratch, from a blank page.

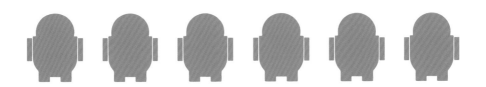

Our goal is to encourage children not to experience technology passively, but to understand it and see it for what it is: a very powerful tool for bringing their ideas to life.

The book is made up of 6 projects that get progressively more difficult, each of which leads to the creation of a computer videogame. The final product will be a simple game, light years away from the epics that the videogame industry produces. It is important to remember that in our case the goal is to practice programming, not to play videogames.

We will begin with an overview that explains in detail how Scratch is used, but the book is designed so that you can also start directly from the first project. At the beginning of each chapter, readers will find an explanation of the game they will be creating and the list of materials to use (available for download from the site indicated on the following page).

Then, the procedure to follow to create the game will be illustrated step by step.

During the project, there will be some boxes (magnifier) defining several key concepts for using Scratch independently, and others that feature in-depth looks at various issues (Did You Know?).

At the end of each project readers will find a challenge, a modification to the game to make on their own; the solution to them can be found at the end of the book. We would advise that all users try to complete these, in order to test themselves and verify how well they have understood what has been taught during the project.

THE SITE

A minisite has been created to support this series, reachable at the address www.coding.whitestar.it.

Here children will find characters and backdrops to customize their projects. Naturally the games work with different images, as long as they have the right format!

On our site you will find all the materials in SVG format, but Scratch also supports PNG, JPG, and GIF.

The materials and games contained in this book and on the website are the property of the Publisher. They may be freely used and reproduced, exclusively for non-commercial purposes.

WHAT DOES PROGRAMMING MEAN?

Programming means giving commands to a computer in a language that it can understand.

A program, therefore, transforms the computer into a tool that is useful for a certain task, by simply telling the machine how it must behave and on what occasion. The commands written by a programmer must be very precise and have to take into account every possibility, because computers don't have the ability to think autonomously!

Algorithms

An algorithm is a precise and ordered series of instructions to obtain a result. Take for example how to explain to a robot how to reach a destination in a grid such as this one. In order to reach C3 starting from A1, the robot could carry out the following steps: move 1 box to the right 2 times. Move up 1 box 2 times. This is a very simple example of an algorithm.

Obviously there is never just one possible solution to a problem!

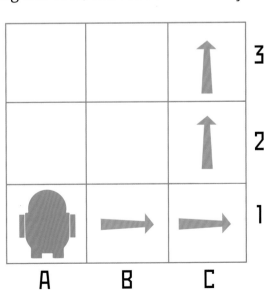

Scratch 2.0

"Scratch is a project of the Lifelong Kindergarten Group at the MIT Media Lab. It is provided free of charge.
Scratch helps young people learn to think creatively, reason systematically, and work collaboratively — essential skills for life in the 21st century.
With Scratch, you can program your own interactive stories, games, and animations — and share your creations with others in the online community."

[https://scratch.mit.edu/about/]

The projects in this book are designed for the version 2.0 of Scratch, but there is also an older version (1.4).
Scratch is not only a programming language: it is also a programming environment, a community, a website, and a cloud platform where users can upload their projects.
There are two ways of using Scratch: you can either use the online editor or download the program on your computer, so that you can use it even without an Internet connection.

ONLINE

To use Scratch online just go to the website scratch.mit.edu and join the Scratch community by creating an account. We suggest helping your children with this part, as personal data will be requested.
After making an account, with the username and password that you have chosen you can log in to your own personal space and start creating.
The projects created remain private, unless you yourself decide to share them.

OFFLINE

To use Scratch offline, you can download the program from the official site: click on the link scratch.mit.edu/scratch2download and follow the instructions for installing it.
There is no need to create an account to use Scratch offline.
In both versions, by clicking on [?] you will find useful suggestions that can help you begin to study, or explore further, the topics discussed in this book.

Adobe AIR

If it is not already installed on your computer, download and install the latest version of **Adobe AIR**

Scratch 2.0 Offline Editor (Beta)

Then download and install the **Scratch 2.0 Offline Editor**

Support materials

Need help getting started? Here are some useful resources.

Starter Projects
Getting Started Guide
Scratch Cards

SPRITES, STAGES, SCRIPTS

SPRITES

The 2D characters and objects that you will use in Scratch are called Sprites. Scratch lets you to choose them from its library, but you can also design them yourself, upload them from your computer, or create them from photos.

x: 240 y: 30

Sprites   New sprite:

STAGES

The Stage in Scratch manages all the backdrops of your projects. Like with the Sprites, you can select backdrops from the library, design them, upload them from your computer, or use a photo.

New backdrop:

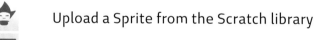 Upload a Sprite from the Scratch library

 Upload a backdrop from the Scratch library

Design your Sprite or your backdrop

Upload your Sprite or your backdrop from the computer

Take a photo from the Webcam to create your Sprite or backdrop

SCRIPTS

Scripts are the instructions and the commands that you give to the Sprites or to the Stage.

SEQUENTIALITY

The computer carries out the commands from the top to the bottom, one at a time.

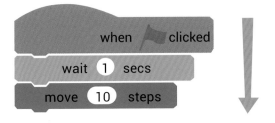

ACTIVE SCRIPT

When Scratch is performing a script, this lights up!

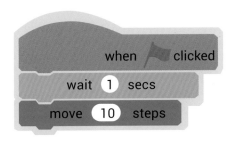

AREAS

Scratch 2.0 is divided into 5 main areas. Let's go through them together.

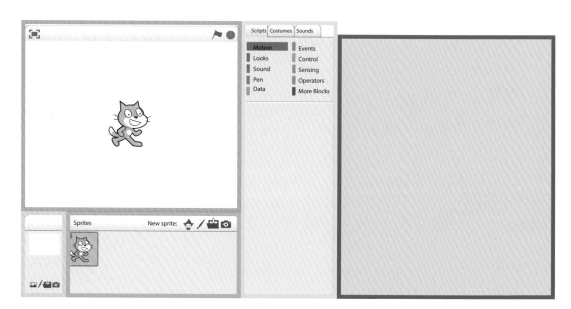

Scene of the game: here is where your stories and games come to life. From this area you can press:

⚐ Start the game.

⬢ Stop the game.

⟦⟧ Activate game mode. Careful! In game mode you can only play, not make changes! To return and make adjustments to the project click on the same key again.

Stage Area: this contains the backdrops of your project

Sprite Area: this contains your characters and objects

Blocks Area: this contains all the commands for Scratch

Scripts Area: is designed to allow you to give commands to each of your backdrops and objects

Tools

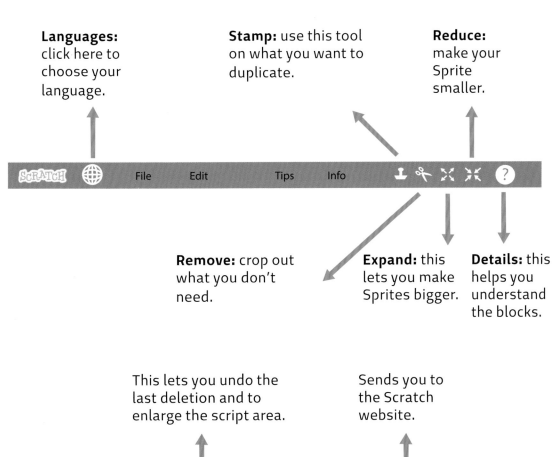

Languages: click here to choose your language.

Stamp: use this tool on what you want to duplicate.

Reduce: make your Sprite smaller.

Remove: crop out what you don't need.

Expand: this lets you make Sprites bigger.

Details: this helps you understand the blocks.

This lets you undo the last deletion and to enlarge the script area.

Sends you to the Scratch website.

To open a project or save one.

This shows a list of projects that are useful to users who are learning to use Scratch, or more experienced users who want more information.

13

Blocks

Hat Blocks: hat blocks are always placed at the start of a script, and indicate where it starts. Nothing can be placed above them.

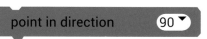

Stack Blocks: these are the blocks that you'll use the most, because they tell the components of the game WHAT they have to do. You can place other blocks above and below them.

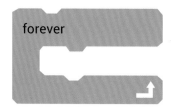

C Blocks: these tell the game IF and HOW MANY TIMES to do something. They come in a C-shape because they can wrap themselves around other blocks.

Cap Blocks: these are placed at the end of a script, and indicate the END. You cannot place any other blocks below them.

Boolean Blocks: standing out due to their hexagonal shapes, these can take on only values: TRUE or FALSE.

Reporter Blocks: these have rounded edges and can be different types of values, for examples numbers or words.

Look closely! In some of these blocks you'll find a little black triangle. If you click on it you'll open what in the computer world is known as a drop-down menu: from you can choose a different value from the one written in the block.

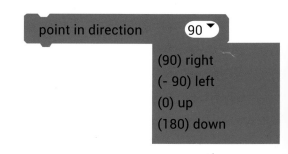

The blocks in Scratch are of different colors according to the category to which they belong. For example: all the commands that make the characters of your projects move are found in the motion category and are blue. In order to see a category's blocks just click on its name.

Motion	Events
Looks	Control
Sound	Sensing
Pen	Operators
Data	More Blocks

The blocks can also be joined to one another, if their form fits in the space you want to place them in.

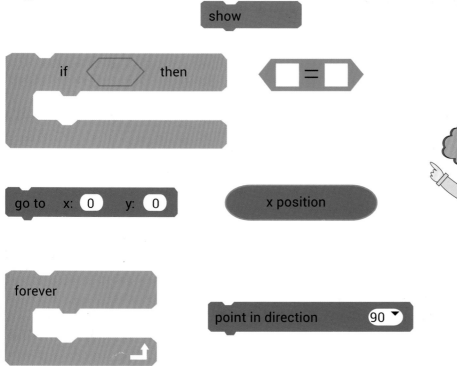

Motion	Events
Looks	Control
Sound	Sensing
Pen	Operators
Data	More Blocks

Motion: these contain the instructions that control your Sprites movement.

Looks: here you'll find the blocks that modify the appearance of everything on the scene.

Sound: want to add a bit of music to your project? You'll find what you need here.

Pen: Whether it's just to draw simple a line or to create complex visual effects, you're going to need a pen!

Data: if you click on this category you can create data. What are they? You'll find out further on!

Event: these include all the blocks that represent events or situations.

Control: the blocks in this extremely important category explain to the program how and when to activate the various scripts.

Sensing: if two objects are touching or if a key is being pressed, the sensing blocks always notice!

Operators: sometimes you need to do some math... Operators can make calculations or compare two numbers.

More blocks: this category is empty but it lets you make your own blocks!

Panes

SPRITES PANES

Each Sprite has 3 panes:
If you select the first, Scripts, it will open the list of the blocks, and to the right the area to construct the Scripts.

The second, Costumes, contains all of the costumes of the Sprite selected, in other words all the ways that Sprite can appear.
To the right you will see Scratch's Paint Editor, which allows you to edit the appearance of the Sprites.

The Sounds pane lets you add a sound from your Scratch library but also to record one or upload one from your computer!

STAGES PANES

The Stage also has 3 panes:
Scripts and Sounds work just like they do with Sprites.
But the second, Backdrops, is different.

Just as Sprites appears differently according to the costume they are wearing at the moment, so too the appearance of the Stage changes according to the backdrop.
If you open the Backdrops pane you'll find all of the ones you have inserted in your project. Of course, you can also add more of them!

PROJECTS

Here's where your adventure into the world
of programming videogames begins.

If you don't have Scratch 2.0 on your computer
ask for help from an adult!

Some of these games might seem easy. . . to play!
The real challenge is programming them,
from the ground up.

1.

LEVEL

SMASH THE MOSQUITO

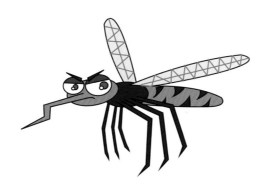

SMASH THE MOSQUITO

LEVEL

Your first game is infested with a very annoying mosquito that buzzes all over your computer screen.

THE GAME

Try to aim for the mosquito with the cursor of your mouse and click to smash it while it moves fast around the screen.

WHAT YOU'LL LEARN:

- To set up a new project
- To program a random movement
- To change the costumes of the Sprites

SPRITES

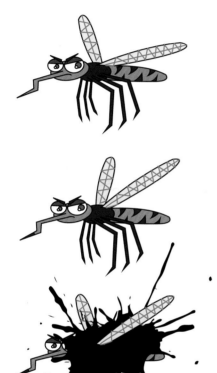

BACKDROPS

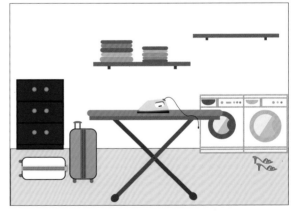

MATERIALS

On the site indicated in the introduction we've prepared everything that you'll need to create our games. You'll find various versions of each Sprite and many backdrops upon which to set their adventures.

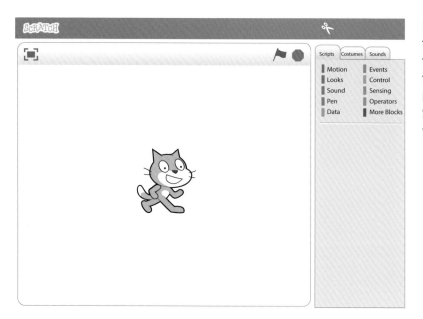

Before starting to program, we have to make sure the tools we'll need are ready. So, let's open Scratch and get to work!

Open Scratch, wait a few seconds and you'll find your first project in front of you.
For now it's just a blank page... or almost blank.
Every time you begin a new project, at the center of the screen you'll find a cat, the Sprite that is the symbol of Scratch.

This time the Scratch Cat won't be a character in your game, so you'll have to delete it by using the tool REMOVE.

CHOOSE A SPRITE

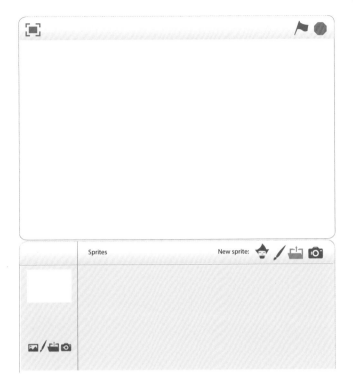

Can you imagine a videogame without characters or objects that move, speak, run, and jump? Impossible, right? So let's see how to choose our first Sprite.

In the section New Sprite, click on the folder icon to upload a SPRITE from your computer, after downloading it from the site.

To learn how to download the Sprite from the site, go back to Chapter 1 of this book.

Choose the mosquito you prefer from the ones you see.

SPRITES

The word Sprite refers to a mythological creature similar to a fairy or a ghost. The characters designed in 2D like the ones we use in Scratch are known as Sprites for the way they glide over fixed image, the backdrop, without being part of it. This way of drawing and animating characters was invented in the 1970s, and made it possible to put more numerous and detailed characters into videogames. Before this innovation, the computer had to redraw the character from scratch every time it moved.

CHOOSE A BACKDROP

The Sprites don't move in a vacuum: every game has a setting.
In this case the mosquito will fly in front of a wall. Like we did before for the Sprite, we have to choose the backdrop from our image library.

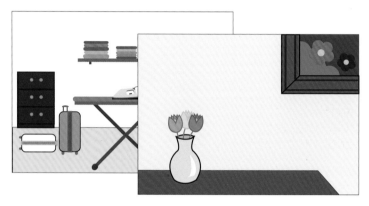

Click on the folder icon, in the section New Backdrop, to upload a BACKDROP from your computer.
Again, remember to download it first from the site.

BACKDROPS

The games we'll be creating with Scratch will almost always be set on fixed images, called Backdrops. As with Sprites, you can choose to draw your own backdrops, get them from somewhere else, upload them from the Scratch library, or add them directly from your computer's camera.

ATTENTION! The Backdrop is not the same thing as the Stage. The stage is an element of Scratch you can give instructions to. With the Stage you can change the backdrop and manage other aspects that don't concern a single Sprite but the game in general.

Every Sprite must always know what to do and when to do it: you're the one who tells it! To begin, let's move to the Script section.

For more info on the Scratch Areas, go to page 12

Drag the first block into the work area: WHEN GREEN FLAG CLICKED. The green flag indicated the start of the game. Under this command you'll put, in order, all the instructions that the Sprite will have to carry out when the program starts up.

Under this, place a block SWITCH TO COSTUME. This way, as soon as the green flag is clicked, the Sprite will take on the appearance you have chosen.

COSTUMES

Sprites' costumes are how they appear. But even if its appearance changes, a Sprite remains itself. Just like you are still yourself even if you change your clothes!

The costumes are all the ways that our Sprites can appear in the game. The cool thing is that, working on a computer, there are no limits to our imagination: a dinosaur can easily turn into an apple at our command. If you want to take advantage of all the potential Scratch offers, you must absolutely learn how to use this tool!

MAKE THE MOSQUITO FLY

The mosquito will need to fly on your screen for the entire duration of the game.

To make sure this happens, let's take a FOREVER loop and put it under the last block we placed.

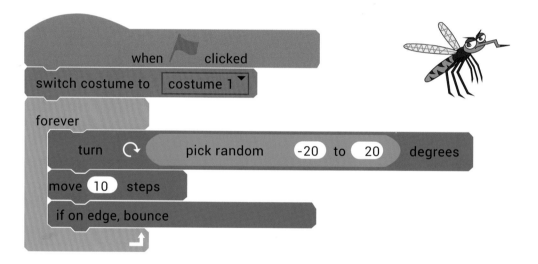

To simulate the mosquito's flight, add inside the FOREVER block some motion commands:
the block TURN... DEGREES will change the direction the mosquito flies in, while MOVE 10 STEPS will make it move.
To make sure the mosquito always chooses a different direction to move in, insert the "operator" PICK RANDOM -20 TO 20 in the blank space between TURN... DEGREES and assign it the values of -20 and 20.
Try to put different numbers, like -10 and 10 and see what happens!

SMASH THE MOSQUITO

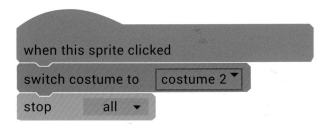

When the mosquito gets smashed – or in this case, clicked – the game ends.

Take the "event" WHEN THIS SPRITE CLICKED, add SWITCH TO COSTUME. . . and choose the name of the second costume for the Sprite.

To finish, use the block STOP ALL to stop the game.

FOREVER

Blocks like FOREVER are known as Loops. Instructions of this kind are used in programming to make a series of commands repeat. In Scratch, a FOREVER repeats the instructions it contains to infinity, in the order they're arranged in. Well... not quite forever, more like until the program is closed.

REMEMBER TO SAVE!

You don't want to lose all the work you've done, do you?

Click on File, then on Save As.
Pick a name to give to your project and where to save it.

From now on you won't need to use the command Save As.
Just click on Save and the computer will save the latest changes.

DID YOU KNOW?

SAVE AS

When you create something with Scratch, or with any program, you have to remember to save it often, so you don't lose your work if something goes wrong.

The first time you do it, you'll have to choose a name to give to your work and where to save it. The next times, you can choose to update the file you're working on (by clicking on File > Save), or to create multiple versions with different names (File > Save As), for example if you want to try out changes you're not sure about.

DID YOU KNOW?

FILES AND FOLDERS

A game, a document, a book, a film, a song... Everything you see on your computer is a file, which is an object made up of information that is read by a program.

A modern computer contains hundreds of thousands of Files: for this reason they are organized into folders, so that they can be found more easily.

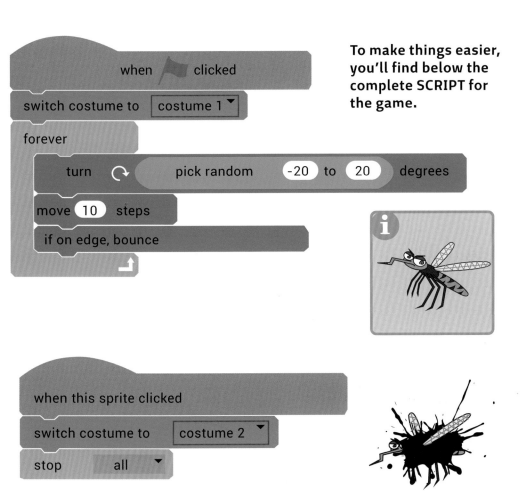

To make things easier, you'll find below the complete SCRIPT for the game.

```
when [flag] clicked
switch costume to [costume 1 ▼]
forever
    turn ↻ (pick random (-20) to (20)) degrees
    move (10) steps
    if on edge, bounce
```

```
when this sprite clicked
switch costume to [costume 2 ▼]
stop [all ▼]
```

SCRIPT

In everyday English, the word "script" refers to what actors read from to learn their lines. In a program, a script is a sequence of instructions used to make it perform tasks. Imagine that all the characters that you insert into Scratch are actors in your game, each with their part to play. Every script, for example the one in the image above, begins with an Event, like WHEN GREEN FLAG CLICKED, and stops with the last instruction given, or when the red light is clicked.

2.

LEVEL

THE
RACETRACK

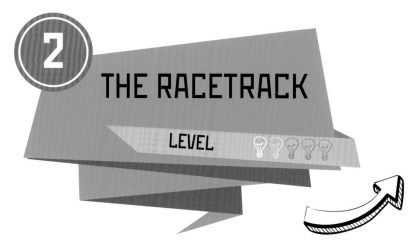

THE RACETRACK

LEVEL

Start your engines, we're off! Reach the finish line as quickly as possible.

THE GAME

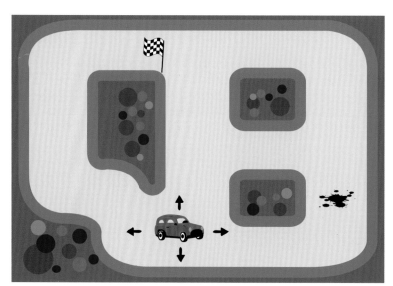

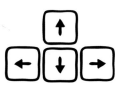

Drive the car with the four arrows keys to get to the end of the racetrack.

WHAT YOU'LL LEARN:

- Interaction between the character and the environment

- Make Sprites speak

34

SPRITES

BACKDROPS

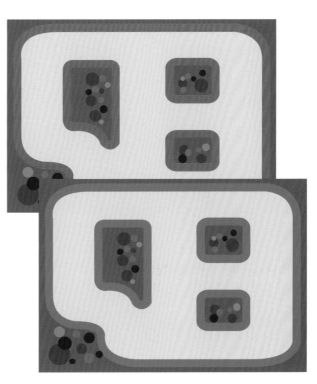

WHY DO WE LOVE PLAYING VIDEOGAMES?

Usually, with the exception of certain very odd cases, we prefer to play a videogame instead of cleaning our room or doing pages of math exercises. It might seem obvious, but have you ever wondered why?

The creators of a videogame work very hard to create the most interesting and exciting experience possible: no easy task! There are people who study and specialize in what is known as game design, which is the art of creating high-quality game experiences.

To Begin

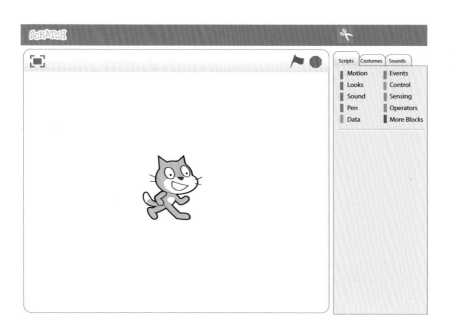

Let's get Scratch ready to work on a new project.

Open Scratch, delete the cat, and give a name to the new project by clicking on FILE > SAVE AS.
Then choose the Sprites and the backdrops you need for the new game.

Choose a Sprite and a Backdrop

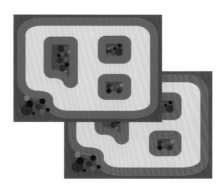

36

A Sprite's Movement

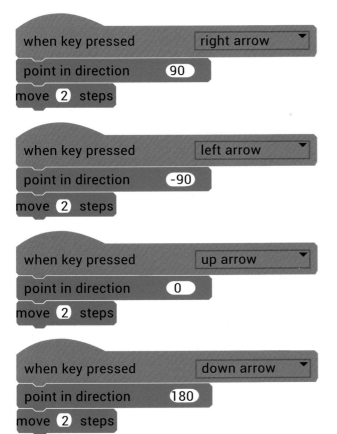

```
when key pressed          right arrow ▼
  point in direction    90
move  2  steps
```

```
when key pressed          left arrow ▼
  point in direction    -90
move  2  steps
```

```
when key pressed          up arrow ▼
  point in direction    0
move  2  steps
```

```
when key pressed          down arrow ▼
  point in direction    180
move  2  steps
```

Whether it's smashing a mosquito or building a city made of cubes, the idea at the basis of every videogame is to interact with a virtual world by performing an action in the real world. In our game, for example, we'll use the arrow keys to make the car move.

Insert the command POINT IN DIRECTION 90 to make the car turn right.
To make it move in that direction, add the block MOVE 2 STEPS.
Place both the blocks under the "Event" WHEN RIGHT ARROW KEY PRESSED.

Do the same for the other three arrows: left, up, and down. Remember to change the direction for each arrow!

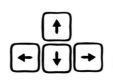

Right: 90
Left: -90
Up: 0
Down: 180

EVENT

Every Script, in order to work, must begin with a starting "Event."
Blocks of the Event category have a different shape than all the others: they have what looks like a hat, because no other commands can be placed on top of them.

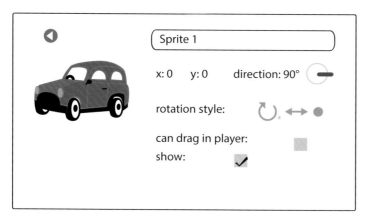

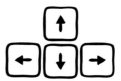

If we try to use the arrow keys we see that the car changes its position according to the direction it's moving.

So if we don't want to travel in an upside-down car, we'll have to solve the problem!

To keep the Sprite from tipping over, change its rotation style!

Click on  and select ⟷

Scratch allows you to give Sprites three rotation styles:

↻ Free: the Sprite rolls freely in all directions.

⟷ Right-Left: the object turns only to the right and to the left.

● Blocked: the object cannot rotate.

START!

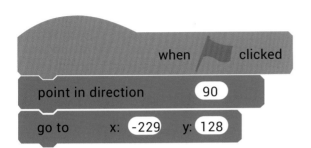

when 🚩 clicked

point in direction **90**

go to x: **-229** y: **128**

At the beginning of the game the car will always have to appear on the starting line. So let's learn how to set a starting position for a Sprite.

The command WHEN GREEN FLAG CLICKED indicates the start of the game. Insert the command POINT IN DIRECTION 90 to make the car turn right.

Drag the car to its starting position, then use the command GO TO X:, Y: to block its position at the start of every race.

The coordinates (X and Y) will automatically be the right ones.

COORDINATES

Every point in game area is identified by two numbers, called "coordinates", X and Y. The X indicated the position on a horizontal line, the Y on a vertical line. The two lines intersect at the center of the screen, in the point called X: 0, Y: 0.

In Scratch you can see the coordinates of the cursor by looking at the bottom right of the stage, while to see the current coordinates of a Sprite you can look at the top right of the screen.

In general, negative coordinates, (with the minus sign) are found below or to the left, while positive ones are above or to the right.

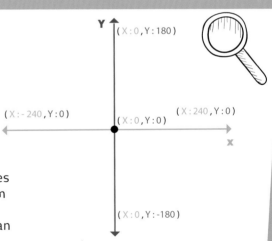

Y (X:0,Y:180)

(X:-240,Y:0)

(X:0,Y:0)

(X:240,Y:0)

X

(X:0,Y:-180)

DON'T GO OFF THE TRACK

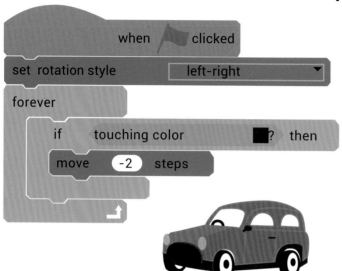

In order to be fun, every game has to have rules. Whoever creates it has to decide what is allowed and what is not.

The car can still go off the track. So players could simply drive in a straight line right to the finish line!

Make it so that the car has to remain on the road.

To create this effect take a command IF. . . THEN: the car will have to turn back, with the command MOVE -2 STEPS, only if it's TOUCHING THE COLOR of the edge of the racetrack.

To choose the right color, click once on the box of the block TOUCHING COLOR and a second time on the color of the edge of the racetrack.

IF. . . THEN

The concept of IF. . . THEN is one of the most important in Scratch, and in programming in general. The words "if" and "then" connect two events, so that if one of these, called the condition, is true, then by necessity the second, the consequence, will also occur. The condition needs to be inserted in the empty hexagonal space of the block, while the consequence is placed in the internal part of the block.

The Finish Line!

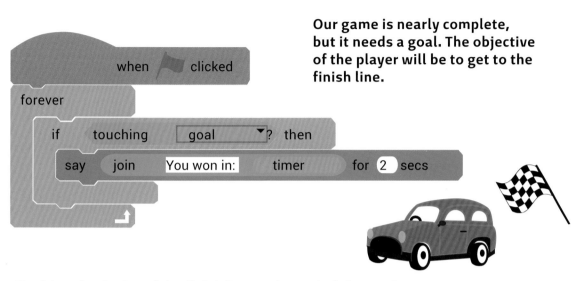

Our game is nearly complete, but it needs a goal. The objective of the player will be to get to the finish line.

```
when [flag] clicked
forever
    if touching [goal ▼]? then
        say join [You won in:] (timer) for (2) secs
```

Position the Sprite of the finish line at the end of the track.
Then build the Script so that IF the car TOUCHING THE FINISH LINE, THEN it will have to SAY for 2 seconds "You won in:" and the time elapsed since the start of the game (timer).

To insert two elements in the blank space of the block SAY you just need to use a JOIN Operator.

Too Easy?

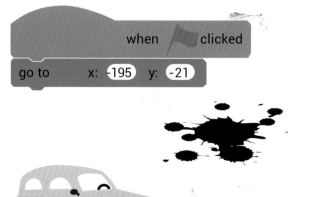

```
when [flag] clicked
go to x: (-195) y: (-21)
```

Add obstacles!

After uploading the Sprite "Oil stain", place it where you want on the racetrack.
Insert the block GO TO X:, Y: to fix the obstacle in that place, WHEN GREEN FLAG CLICKED.

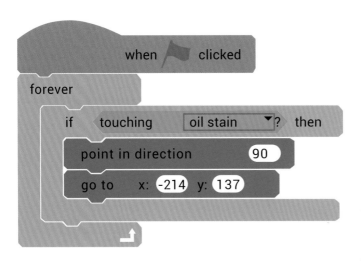

We have added a new element: now to reach the finish line players will have to watch out for obstacles.

Each time the car touches an obstacle, it will be repositioned at the beginning of the track.

Construct the IF. . . THEN block by placing in its hexagonal space the Sensing block TOUCHING "Oil stain."

Then add the command POINT IN DIRECTION and a GO to X:, Y: identical to the ones you used for the starting line (page 39).

Remember to save your work by going to FILE > SAVE AS so you don't lose all the work you have coded!

To help you, here's the complete SCRIPT for the game.

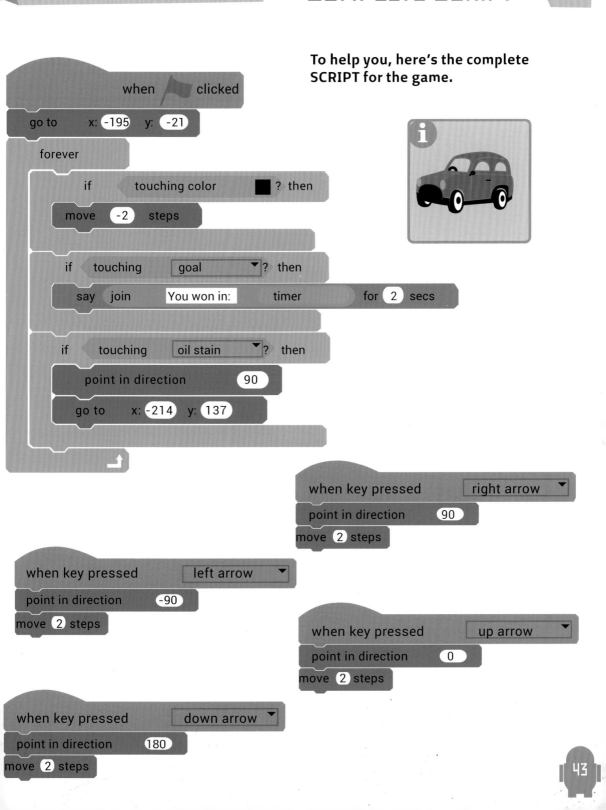

when 🏁 clicked

go to x: -195 y: -21

forever

  if touching color ⬛ ? then

    move -2 steps

  if touching goal ▼ ? then

    say join You won in: timer for 2 secs

  if touching oil stain ▼ ? then

    point in direction 90

    go to x: -214 y: 137

when key pressed right arrow ▼
point in direction 90
move 2 steps

when key pressed left arrow ▼
point in direction -90
move 2 steps

when key pressed up arrow ▼
point in direction 0
move 2 steps

when key pressed down arrow ▼
point in direction 180
move 2 steps

43

CHALLENGE

44

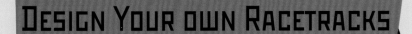

DESIGN YOUR OWN RACETRACKS

Scratch lets you design your own Backdrops and Sprites.

Try to customize this game by making a backdrop on your own.
It doesn't necessarily have to be a circle.

A hint:

Remember to make the edges of the racetrack all the same color.

3.

LEVEL

CATCH ME
IF YOU CAN!

CATCH ME IF YOU CAN!

LEVEL

Zeno the alien has been sent to Earth to carry out a secret mission, but he's enjoying himself so much that he doesn't want to go back!

Help him escape from the spaceship that wants to take him home!

THE GAME

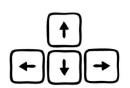

Move Zeno using the 4 arrows to keep him from being taken by the spaceship.

WHAT YOU'LL LEARN:

- To control the interaction between characters better

- To program a random movement

MATERIALS

SPRITES

BACKDROPS

WHY DON'T WE ALL PLAY THE SAME GAMES?

A good game must, first of all, make us want to play it. But not everyone has fun in the same way! Experts in game design have therefore classified players on the basis of what they look for in a game.

Do they want novelty and adventure, or do they prefer to know exactly what awaits them? Are they looking for a tough challenge that calls for all their reflexes and patience, or do they simply want to relax? When you invent a videogame, remember to think about the players first!

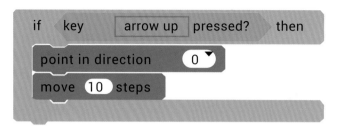

We have already seen an easy way to program a Sprite to move when a key is pressed.

But as you probably noticed, the response is a bit slow. Luckily in programming there is never just one way of doing something!

Insert the commands that make a Sprite move and turn into an IF-THEN block.
In the empty space between the words IF and THEN, place a KEY PRESSED sensing block.

This way the program will check whether the player is pressing the key indicated: in this case, the character will move in the direction chosen.

DIRECTION

Scratch measures direction in degrees. A Sprite that looks up is pointing in direction 0. If it turns to the right, making a right angle, it will be direction 90. If it faces down the direction will be 180.

To make a Sprite face left you'll have to use a negative number, that is, a number with a minus in front of it, from -179 to 0, as indicated by the blue arrow. Vice versa, to make the Sprite face a point to the right, you'll need to use a positive number from 0 to 180, as indicated by the red arrow.

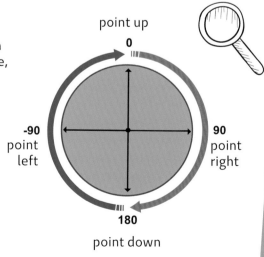

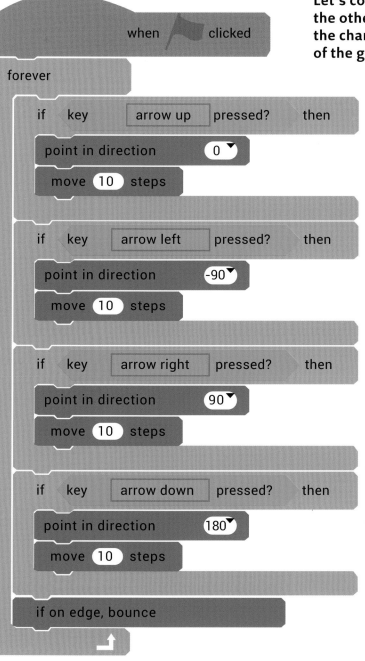

when 🚩 clicked

forever

  if   key   arrow up   pressed?   then

    point in direction   0

    move 10 steps

  if   key   arrow left   pressed?   then

    point in direction   -90

    move 10 steps

  if   key   arrow right   pressed?   then

    point in direction   90

    move 10 steps

  if   key   arrow down   pressed?   then

    point in direction   180

    move 10 steps

  if on edge, bounce

Let's continue programming the other directions, and stopping the character from going out of the game area.

We repeat the procedure, associating a direction to each key. Then we insert all the script into a FOREVER loop to make sure it works for the entire game.

Then, inside the FOREVER block (but outside of the IF-THENs!), place a block IF ON EDGE, BOUNCE to keep Zeno from going off the screen, and thus getting away not only from his pursuers, but from us as well!

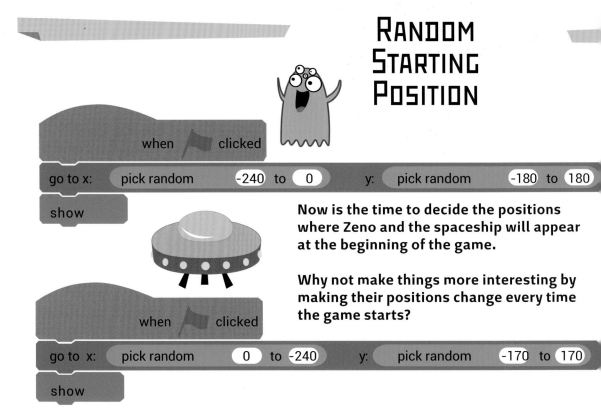

RANDOM STARTING POSITION

when 🚩 clicked

go to x: (pick random (-240) to (0)) y: (pick random (-180) to (180))

show

Now is the time to decide the positions where Zeno and the spaceship will appear at the beginning of the game.

Why not make things more interesting by making their positions change every time the game starts?

when 🚩 clicked

go to x: (pick random (0) to (-240)) y: (pick random (-170) to (170))

show

Do you remember how to assign a starting position to a Sprite?
We did it in game 2, The Racetrack.

Start by inserting the block GO TO X:, Y:.
This time, however, the X and Y have to change every time the game starts.

Drag into the work area two PICK RANDOM NUMBER blocks, taking them from the OPERATORS category, and insert them into the spaces of X and Y.

To make sure that Zeno and the spaceship don't appear too close to one another, we'll assign to each of them one half of the screen.
For Zeno, we'll choose an interval that places him on the left side of the screen, whereas for the spaceship we'll select coordinates that keep it on the other side.

To finish, add a block SHOW: the reason for this last block will become clear later.

It's time to give life to the spaceship, programming it so that it chases after Zeno.

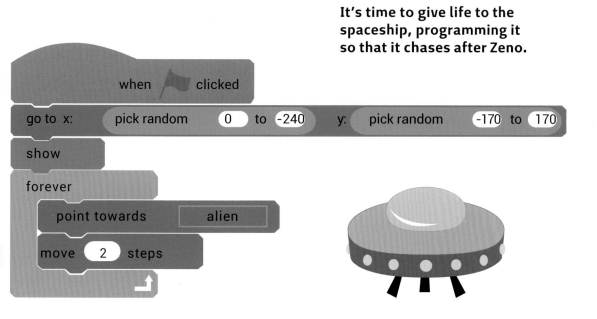

We'll insert a POINT TOWARDS block in a FOREVER loop, and choose Zeno from the drop-down menu.

This way the spaceship will always be turned towards our character. At this point we'll add a block of MOVE. . . STEPS to make the spaceship come towards us.

Remember to set a number of steps for the spaceship that is less than the steps set for Zeno, otherwise the game will be impossible to play!

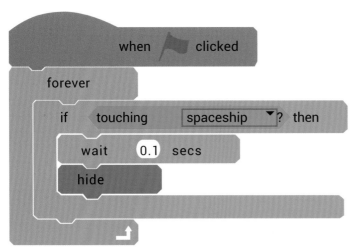

Now that both Zeno and the spaceship are moving, it's time to create the actual structure of the game.

Let's start by making Zeno disappear if the spaceship manages to catch him.

Take an IF. . . THEN block and put the TOUCHING sensing block in the hexagonal space for the condition.

Open the drop-down menu by clicking on the little black arrow and choose the spaceship's name. Then add inside the IF. . . THEN, as a consequence of the collision, the block HIDE.

Before making the Sprite hide, add the block WAIT 0.1 SECONDS to make sure the collision takes place correctly.

Did You Know?

COLLISION

Collision is how programmers call a clash between two objects in the world of a game. Collisions aren't just the spectacular crashes of spaceships or falling helicopters: even if we just want the spaceship to capture Zeno, we need the program to notice that the two objects are touching. Then we get to decide what happens as a consequence.

In Scratch we can use TOUCHING blocks to do this, but WATCH OUT! If the Sprite is a strange shape, the program might have difficulty in accurately detecting the collision.

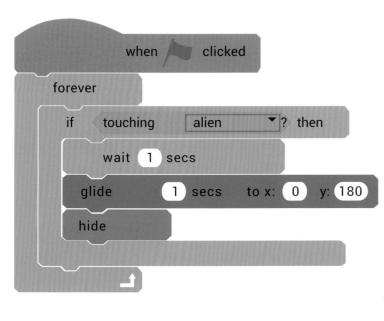

When the spaceship manages to catch the fugitive, it will fly away to return home.

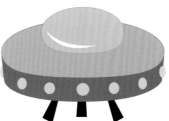

Let's build the script in this way:
IF the spaceship is TOUCHING the alien,
it will have to GLIDE IN 1 SECOND TO X: 0, Y: 180.
These coordinates indicate the center of the upper part of the screen.

Once the spaceship has arrived to the top, it will disappear thanks to the block HIDE.

Remember to save your work by going to FILE > SAVE AS so you don't lose everything you've coded!

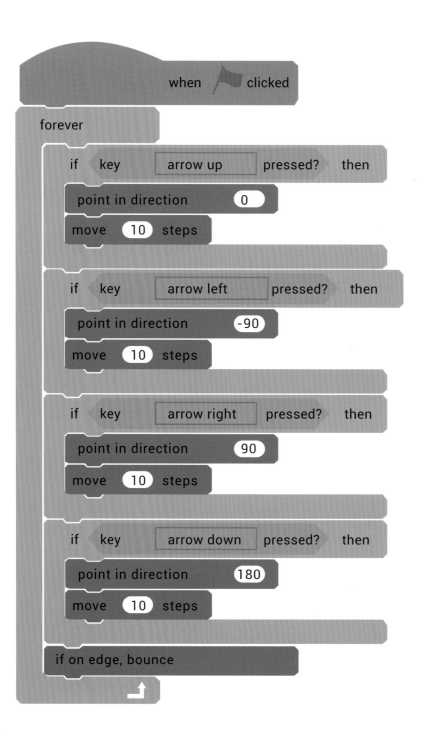

when ⚑ clicked

forever

　if ⟨ key (arrow up) pressed? ⟩ then

　　point in direction (0)

　　move (10) steps

　if ⟨ key (arrow left) pressed? ⟩ then

　　point in direction (-90)

　　move (10) steps

　if ⟨ key (arrow right) pressed? ⟩ then

　　point in direction (90)

　　move (10) steps

　if ⟨ key (arrow down) pressed? ⟩ then

　　point in direction (180)

　　move (10) steps

　if on edge, bounce

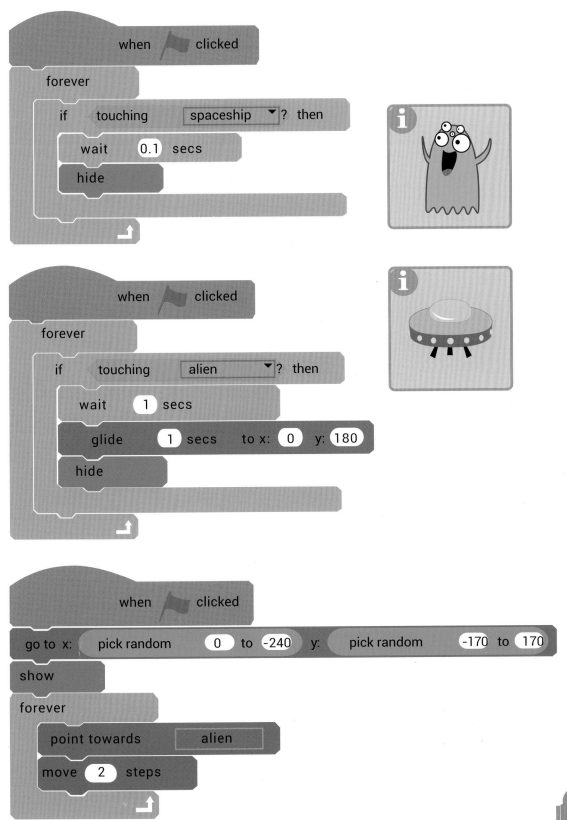

when ⚑ clicked

forever

if touching [spaceship ▼] ? then

wait 0.1 secs

hide

when ⚑ clicked

forever

if touching [alien ▼] ? then

wait 1 secs

glide 1 secs to x: 0 y: 180

hide

when ⚑ clicked

go to x: pick random 0 to -240 y: pick random -170 to 170

show

forever

point towards alien

move 2 steps

CHALLENGE

58

ROLE REVERSAL

Why not invert the parts?

Try to reprogram the game
to play as the spaceship
instead of the alien.

A hint:

Be careful, it's not enough just
to invert the scripts of the Sprites!

4.

LEVEL

EVERYBODY TO THE SEASIDE

4

EVERYBODY TO THE SEASIDE

LEVEL

Packing your bags is hard work. Especially if you have to do it by catching flippers, diver's masks and bathing suits as they fall from the sky!

THE GAME

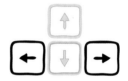

Controlling Milo with the arrow keys, you'll have to catch clothes, bathing suits, flippers, and everything he needs for a summer at the seaside.

Careful not to drop anything!

WHAT YOU'LL LEARN:

- To manage the score of a game through variables

- To create new Events, with messages

SPRITES

BACKDROPS

WHAT ARE RULES FOR?

The creator of a game has complete control over the rules of its world. So why don't we create invincible protagonists, silly enemies and a smooth road to the final goal?

As we have already said, a game must amuse, entertain, and excite. Without obstacles, difficulty, and danger, our adventure would be really quiet boring! The rules are the basis on which the whole gaming experience is built.

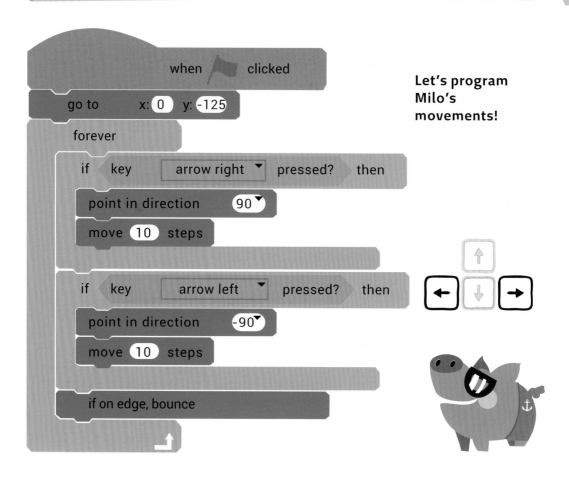

Let's program Milo's movements!

After giving him a starting position with the block GO TO X: Y:, we'll program Milo to move with the arrow keys.

The little pig will only be able to move to the right and to the left, so we will only need these two arrows. Remember to change the Sprite's rotation style (if you don't remember how, go back to Chapter 2).

To make sure Milo doesn't go out of the game area, add the command IF ON EDGE, BOUNCE inside the FOREVER loop.

POSITIONING THE OBJECTS

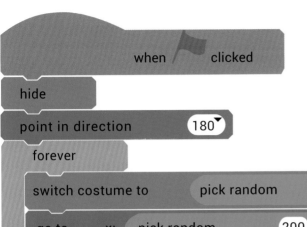

Before falling from up high, the objects will need to have a costume and be placed at the point they'll fall from. It's important that the player not see this phase!

when 🏁 clicked
hide
point in direction 180 ▾
forever
  switch costume to pick random 1 to 6
  go to x: pick random 200 to -200 y: 180
  show

In a movie, no one would want to see the technicians and the director preparing the scene!

First of all, let's order the Sprite to hide and face downwards.

At this point let's make it so that it randomly chooses one of its costumes: this way, using only one Sprite, we'll be able to make different objects fall.

Then we'll position the Sprite in the upper part of the game area at a point that is always different.

Now that everything is ready, our object can enter the scene with the command SHOW.

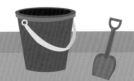

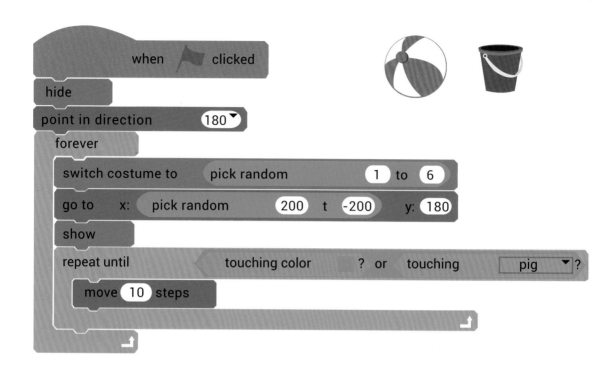

when ⚑ clicked

hide

point in direction (180 ▾)

forever

switch costume to (pick random (1) to (6))

go to x: (pick random (200) t (-200)) y: (180)

show

repeat until ◁ touching color ▢ ? or touching (pig ▾) ? ▷

move (10) steps

Work inside the FOREVER loop you've already created. In a REPEAT UNTIL loop, insert the block MOVE 10 STEPS. Now the program will want to know until when to carry out this command. By inserting a logic operator OR in the empty space, you can make the loop end either when our object is touching the color of the grass, OR when it is touching Milo!

LOGIC OPERATORS

To understand what they do, pay attention to these examples (AND, OR, NOT). You'll realize that you use them in everyday life too.

AND: "If we get a cat AND a dog, I'll be happy." The "AND" operator makes the statement "I'll be happy" true only if we get a cat AND a dog (both!).

OR: "If we get a cat OR a dog, I'll be happy," the operator OR makes the statement "I'll be happy" true if we take EITHER the dog OR the cat (only one!).

NOT: "We won't get a pet." This operator inverts the statement: the phrase is true only if we do NOT get an animal.

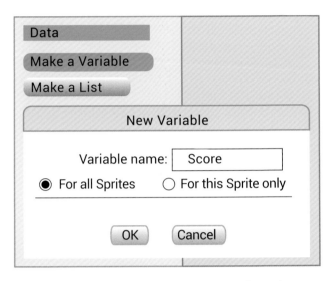

Scoring is an important element of many games, because it gives players a goal and a clear measurement of how good they are. By learning to create a scoring system, we'll discover about one of the most important concepts in programming: variables.

The score is a piece of information that changes during the game and is kept track of by the computer. At the beginning we will have 0 points, but each object we catch will earn us 1 point.

In the category DATA, click on CREATE A VARIABLE.

Give it a name; since in this case it will be a scoring system, it can be called "score." Since the score has to do with the whole game and not just one Sprite, set the variable FOR ALL SPRITES.

In the same way, create another variable that represents the number of objects we miss. We'll call this second variable "lost."

VARIABLES

Let's take a simple example: what is your age? Naturally, you won't have any difficulty answering this question. This is because ever since you were little you have memorized a piece of information (a variable), called "my age," which represents in numerical form the years that have passed since you were born. A variable, as the name suggests, can vary: your age changes every time it's your birthday, but it's always "your age."

In a videogame, a great deal of information must be memorized as variables, for instance the health of the character, their level of experience, the speed at which they move, the lives they have left. . .

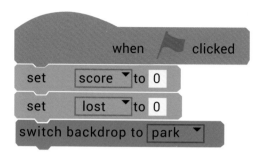

We can also give commands to the Stage! When does it make sense to do so? On two occasions: when it's necessary to go from one backdrop to another, and when we have to give commands not just to one Sprite, but to the entire game. In this case, for example, the stage will manage our two variables.

When the green flag is clicked and the game begins, the variables SCORE and LOST must always have a value of 0. We set this value by using one of the blocks that, at this point, will have appeared in the category DATA: SET variable TO. . .
This command will give a fixed value to the variable indicated.

Lastly, we have to decide what the initial backdrop of the game will be, by adding the block SWITCH TO BACKDROP under the previous commands.

DID YOU KNOW?

INITIALIZATION

Variables don't reset themselves alone: therefore, a player who begins a new game will find the score of the previous game!
To make sure this doesn't happen, it's important that the programmer remembers to initialize each variable, which means explaining to the game what value they must have at the beginning of the game.

COLLISIONS

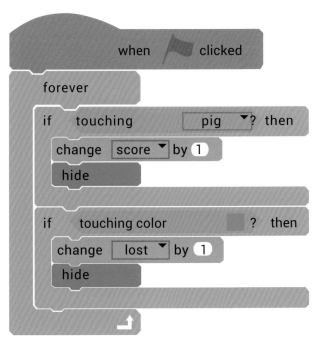

Now we must make the scoring and lost object counter work.

The former will go up by 1 point every time Milo catches an object, the latter will go up by 1 whenever an object lands on the ground.

This is how you can construct these two IF. . . THEN conditional commands. You'll notice that the block CHANGE variable BY. . . always adds the number indicated to the value of the variable. In this case, it will always add 1 point for every collision between Milo and the object.

The LOST variable will also increase by 1, every time an object touches the color of the grass.

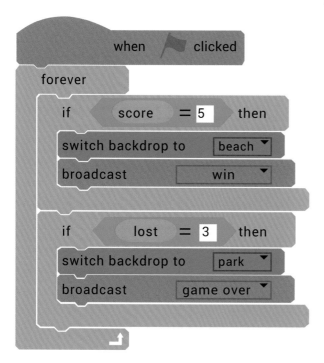

Whether you're winning or losing, the game's got to end sometime! All that remains is for us to decide when.

Construct two IF. . . THENs, one for each possible outcome.
In the first case you have to manage winning:
so IF the variable SCORE is EQUAL to 5,
the backdrop will change to "WIN."

In the second case instead set the conditions for losing:
IF the counter of the LOST objects reaches 3, then the player has lost,
and the backdrop will remain the same.

It would be convenient if winning and losing were actual Events. That way all the actors on the scene would know what to do in one case or the other: the Sprites could disappear, the backdrop could change, you name it!

But how? Simple: by sending a MESSAGE to the whole game, informing each Sprite and the Stage that an event has occurred. When the Sprites and Stage receive this message, they can act or just listen.

MESSAGES

The Stage and the Sprites can communicate with each other using messages. A message is sent by an actor with the block BROADCAST, and it can be used as a condition to start another Script with the block WHEN I RECEIVE. You'll find all of these blocks in the Events category.

To send a message, just open the drop-down menu of the block BROADCAST and choose the option NEW MESSAGE. At this point you can send it, after giving it a name: ideally you would give it a name that is in line with what the message is communicating. But don't worry too much about this name: the player will never see it, as it's only used by you and the program to manage an event inside the game.

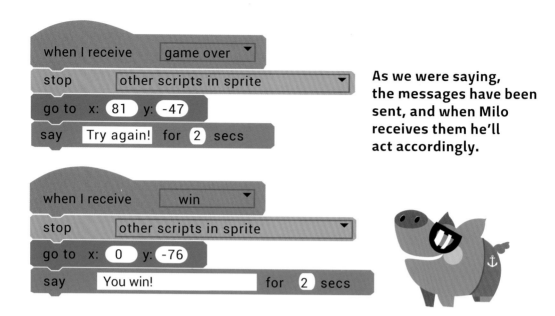

As we were saying, the messages have been sent, and when Milo receives them he'll act accordingly.

Take two WHEN I RECEIVE blocks and set, for each, one of the two possibilities: win and game over.
In both cases, the first thing Milo will have to do is STOP ALL his OTHER SCRIPTS. This way it will no longer be possible to move him with the arrows.
Then he will go to a specific point of the Stage in the case of a win, and to another in the case of a loss, and will say two different phrases according to the Event.

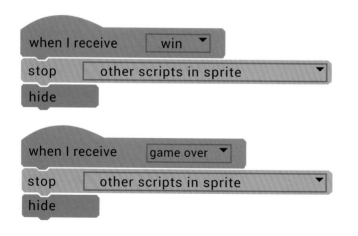

In the same way, when the objects receive the two messages, they will have to hide.

COMPLETE SCRIPT

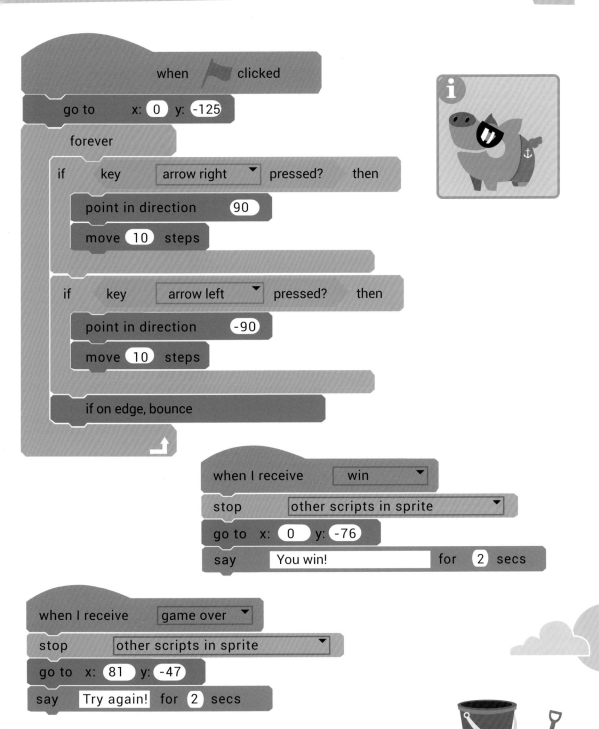

```
when [flag] clicked
go to x: 0 y: -125
forever
    if key [arrow right ▼] pressed? then
        point in direction 90
        move 10 steps

    if key [arrow left ▼] pressed? then
        point in direction -90
        move 10 steps

    if on edge, bounce
```

```
when I receive [win ▼]
stop [other scripts in sprite ▼]
go to x: 0 y: -76
say [You win!] for 2 secs
```

```
when I receive [game over ▼]
stop [other scripts in sprite ▼]
go to x: 81 y: -47
say [Try again!] for 2 secs
```

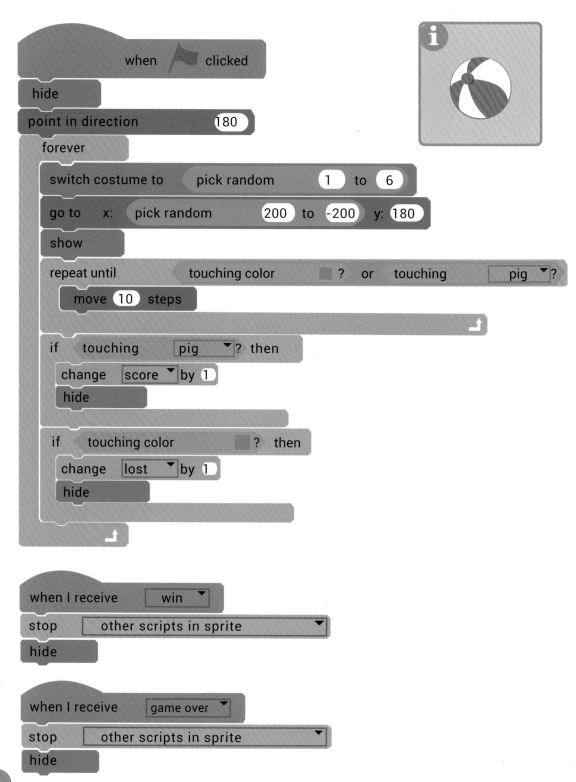

when 🏳 clicked

hide

point in direction 180

forever

switch costume to pick random 1 to 6

go to x: pick random 200 to -200 y: 180

show

repeat until touching color ? or touching pig ?

move 10 steps

if touching pig ? then

change score by 1

hide

if touching color ? then

change lost by 1

hide

when I receive win

stop other scripts in sprite

hide

when I receive game over

stop other scripts in sprite

hide

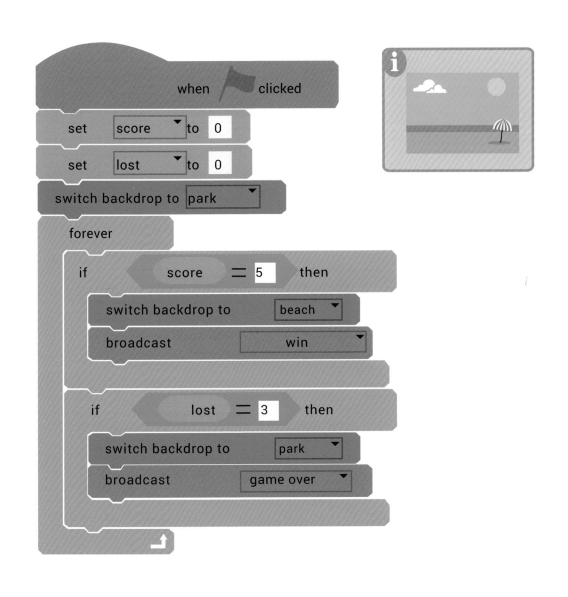

when 🚩 clicked

set score to 0

set lost to 0

switch backdrop to park

forever

if score = 5 then

switch backdrop to beach

broadcast win

if lost = 3 then

switch backdrop to park

broadcast game over

CHALLENGE

MILO SPEAKS!

Before beginning to play, the player has to know what to do. Make it so that Milo himself explains!

Try to make the game begin,
after a brief introduction by Milo
who explains how it works,
when the space bar is pressed.

A hint:

Try using Messages!

5.

LEVEL

THE CRAZY UMBRELLA

5

THE CRAZY UMBRELLA

LEVEL

It would be quite a problem if, on a rainy day, your umbrella came to life and started flying about here and there, don't you think?

THE GAME

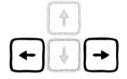

Move with the right and left arrow keys to try to remain under the umbrella:

last 60 seconds without getting too wet in order to win.

WHAT YOU'LL LEARN:

- Clones: how to create, manage, and eliminate them

MATERIALS

SPRITES

BACKDROPS

EASY OR HARD?

If a game is too easy, the player gets bored quickly.

But if it's too hard, the player gets frustrated and the game stops being fun.

Whoever creates a videogame has to be able to balance its level of difficulty.

A good way to do this is to make the game more difficult as time goes on, so that a player who has learned the rules and has become more skilled, doesn't get bored.

THE MAIN CHARACTER'S MOVEMENT

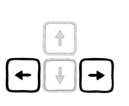

The main character of this game, always starting from the same place, will move under the control of the right and left arrows.

 This is the easy part: you just need the same scripts you used to make Milo move in Chapter 4!

THE MAIN CHARACTER'S LIVES

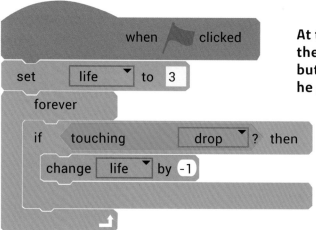

At the beginning of the game the character will have 3 lives, but he'll lose one every time he gets wet.

 First you must create the variable "life."
If you don't remember how to create variables, go back and review it in the previous chapter!

Using and editing the block SET LIFE TO, decide how many lives to give to the character, and therefore how many mistakes the player is allowed to make.

Now drag into the work area a block of IF...THEN and construct it like this:
IF the character is TOUCHING the sprite DROP,
THEN the variable LIFE has to CHANGE BY -1.

THE UMBRELLA'S MOVEMENT

The umbrella has to move unpredictably, but only to the right and to the left.

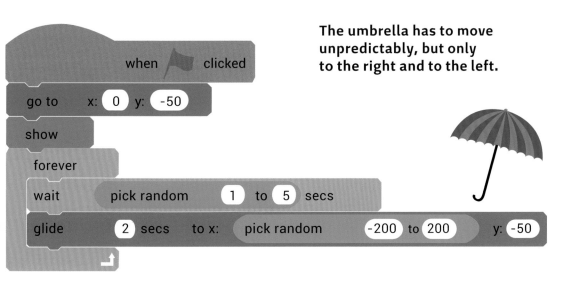

As soon as the game begins, the umbrella has to put itself in its starting position and show itself: the coordinates X: 0, Y: -50 indicate a point at the center of the screen, slightly low.

If you want to review X and Y coordinates go back the "Racetrack" game!

At this point it will be ready to SHOW itself and to start carrying out its task: WAIT for a RANDOM NUMBER of SECONDS and start gliding from right to left (X randomly from -200 to 200), maintaining its Y position unvaried.

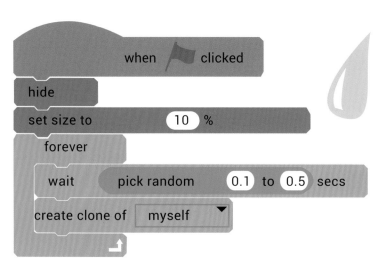

Can you count the drops that fall from the sky when it rains? We couldn't possibly insert into Scratch a Sprite for every drop!

For this reason we will use a single Sprite, but we'll use a special command to create many copies of it, to make the rain more realistic.

The first thing the raindrop Sprite has to do when the game begins is hide. In fact, he won't be the one to show up at all, it will be his clones.

Right after the block HIDE, add a SET SIZE TO 10%, changing it from the number 100 of the original block. In this way the clone will be much smaller than the original, as small as. . . a raindrop.

We're ready for the cloning! In a FOREVER loop insert the command CREATE CLONE OF MYSELF.
With this command alone, however, there'll be a downpour.

To make it rain a bit less, let's make it so that before being created the clones have to WAIT a RANDOM NUMBER from 0.1 TO 0.5 SECONDS.

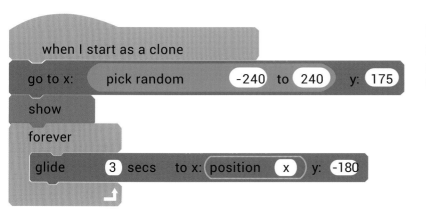

Now that the clones have been created, they have to fall from the sky.

In the category Control you'll find a block called WHEN I START AS A CLONE. Use it to set the behavior of every clone.

Every time a clone is formed, it will have to move up high, to a random point, and appear. Remember how to do it? We've already done it in the game "Everybody to the Seaside."

After that it will have to glide FOREVER downwards, where Y is -180, maintaining its X position so that it falls straight.

CLONES

Scratch gives us the possibility to clone Sprites, that is, to duplicate them. There are 3 main blocks to manage clones:

1. CREATE CLONE OF. . . : this block creates a clone of the Sprite chosen, most of the time it will be MYSELF, the Sprite in which the block is inserted.

2. WHEN I START AS A CLONE: this is a starting Event, it lets us control everything that will happen to the clone as soon as it is created.

3. DELETE THIS CLONE: it's important to delete clones when they are no longer needed; Scratch can manage a maximum of around 300 clones: once this number is exceeded, it stops producing them to avoid making the program too heavy.

THE END OF A CLONE

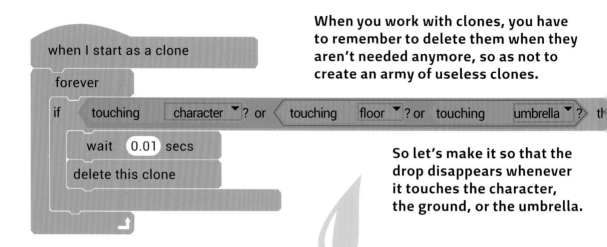

When you work with clones, you have to remember to delete them when they aren't needed anymore, so as not to create an army of useless clones.

So let's make it so that the drop disappears whenever it touches the character, the ground, or the umbrella.

Drag into the work area two. . . OR. . . Operators and place one inside the other like in the image. If you have done it correctly, you'll now have three spaces.

Use this block as the condition inside an IF...THEN. In each of the spaces insert the block TOUCHING + the name of the other three Sprites onscreen. In this way, if it touches any of the three Sprites, the clone will be deleted, but first it must wait 0.01 seconds: otherwise the character won't have time to realize that he is touching the drop and so he won't lose a life.

Remember to put the IF...THEN inside a FOREVER loop. Like before, it is the clone that has to check whether it is touching something, so put the entire script under a block of WHEN I AM CLONED.

THE REFEREE

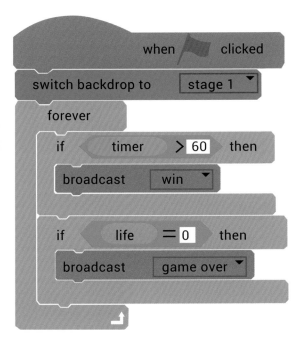

Who will check whether the player wins or loses? We need a ref: an impartial actor who observes the mechanisms of the game. As we have already seen, the Stage is perfect for this role! In this game, you win by lasting 60 seconds!

First let's set a backdrop, which will appear as soon as the green flag is clicked, by using the block SWITCH TO BACKDROP. Starting from this moment the game will count to 60 with the TIMER in Scratch.

IF they get to the end without losing all of their lives, THEN the Stage will broadcast the message "Win."
IF, on the other hand, the lives reach 0, it will broadcast the message "Game Over."

Go back to the previous chapter if you need to review messages.

TIMER

Scratch's Timer starts when the green flag is clicked.
To see the timer onscreen, go to the category Sensing and click on the box next to the TIMER block.
When, in a game, you need to check the timer it's important to use the operators > and <, and not =. This is because time changes quickly, it is difficult for the program to find the exact moment in which the timer is at 60 seconds exactly, but it will surely notice when 60 seconds have gone by, even by a thousandth of a second.

WINNING AND LOSING

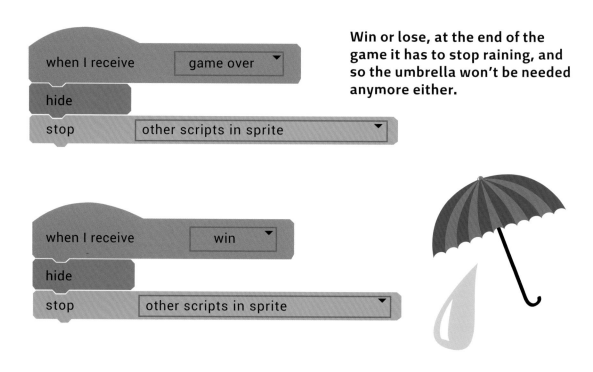

Win or lose, at the end of the game it has to stop raining, and so the umbrella won't be needed anymore either.

when I receive ▸ game over ▾

hide

stop ▸ other scripts in sprite ▾

when I receive ▸ win ▾

hide

stop ▸ other scripts in sprite ▾

Take two blocks of WHEN I RECEIVE and set the game over message for one and the win message for the other.
Under each of the two Events put a HIDE block and STOP... from the drop-down menu of the latter, choose OTHER SCRIPTS IN SPRITE.

Remember to give these instructions both to the Sprite of the raindrop and to the one of the umbrella!

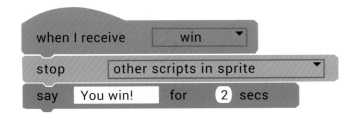

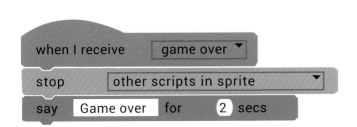

Say something different to the character according to whether the game ends in victory or defeat.

Like before, under the blocks WHEN I RECEIVE WIN and GAME OVER, add STOP OTHER SCRIPTS IN SPRITE.

After that insert a block of SAY... FOR... SECS
and choose what to say to the character in each of the two events!

NON-NUMERIC VARIABLES

As we have already mentioned, variables are information the computer memorizes and which can change during the game, such as the score or the lives remaining. Not all variable are numbers, however!

Also what we write in a SAY block (including the spaces) is actually variable of a particular sort, called "strings." When you write in one of these blocks, the computer receives the command to insert what you have written into a dialogue bubble.

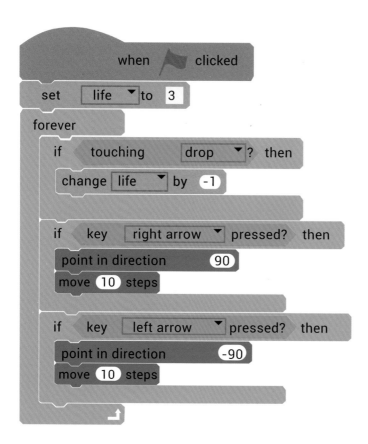

when 🏳 clicked
set life to 3
forever
  if touching drop ? then
    change life by -1

  if key right arrow pressed? then
    point in direction 90
    move 10 steps

  if key left arrow pressed? then
    point in direction -90
    move 10 steps

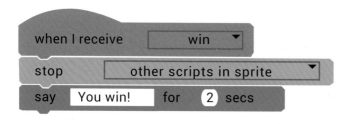

when I receive win
stop other scripts in sprite
say You win! for 2 secs

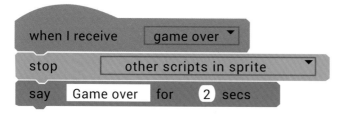

when I receive game over
stop other scripts in sprite
say Game over for 2 secs

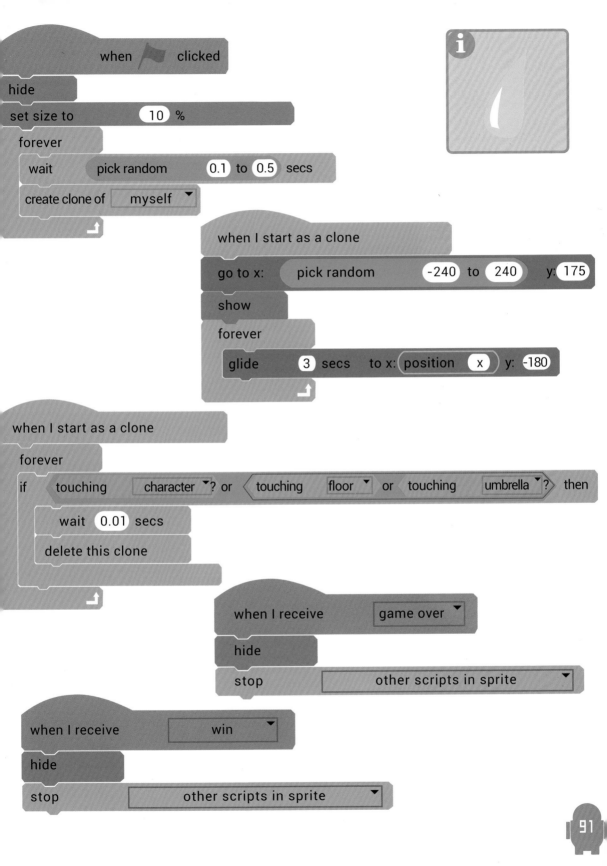

when 🏳 clicked

hide

set size to 10 %

forever

  wait pick random 0.1 to 0.5 secs

  create clone of myself ▾

when I start as a clone

  go to x: pick random -240 to 240 y: 175

  show

  forever

    glide 3 secs to x: position x y: -180

when I start as a clone

forever

  if touching character ▾? or touching floor ▾ or touching umbrella ▾? then

    wait 0.01 secs

    delete this clone

when I receive game over ▾

hide

stop other scripts in sprite ▾

when I receive win ▾

hide

stop other scripts in sprite ▾

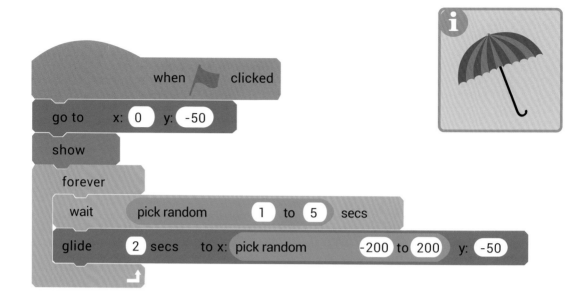

when ⚑ clicked
go to x: `0` y: `-50`
show
forever
  wait pick random `1` to `5` secs
  glide `2` secs to x: pick random `-200` to `200` y: `-50`

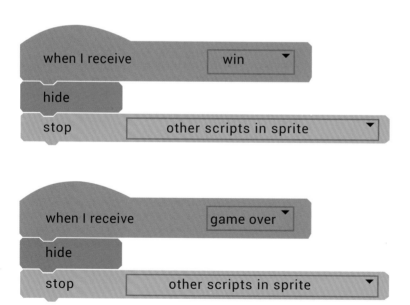

when I receive `win`
hide
stop `other scripts in sprite`

when I receive `game over`
hide
stop `other scripts in sprite`

when 🚩 clicked
switch backdrop to stage 1 ▼
forever
  if timer > 60 then
    broadcast win ▼
  if life = 0 then
    broadcast game over ▼

when I receive win ▼
switch backdrop to stage 2 ▼
stop other scripts in sprite ▼

when I receive game over ▼
switch backdrop to stage 3 ▼
stop other scripts in sprite ▼

CHALLENGE

94

IT'S POURING RAIN!

**Sometimes it sprinkles,
sometimes it pours. . .**

Try to make it rain harder
in the second half of the game.

A hint:

Use the timer!

6.
LEVEL

JELLYFISH SALAD

JELLYFISH SALAD

LEVEL

Catch all the ingredients you need to make the delicious jellyfish salad that turtles love to eat.

THE GAME

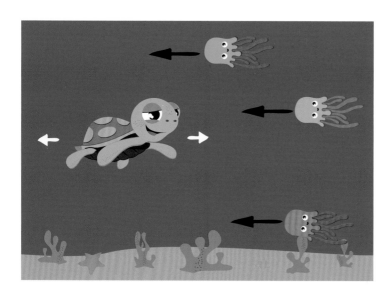

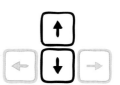

Move the turtle with the up and down arrows to catch all the jellyfish he needs, no more and no less. Attention: in every game the proportions of the ingredients will change!

WHAT YOU'LL LEARN:

- To program a game that runs horizontally

- To make the objective of the game change each time to create an experience that is always different

Materials

Sprites

Backdrops

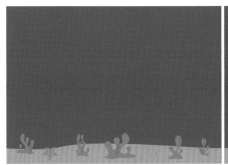

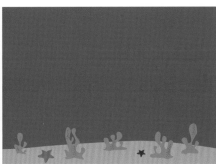

Why Set Goals?

A good game must always give players a reason to play one more game, to play for those famous "5 more minutes."

There are many ways to do this: push the player to show that he or she is better than the others, tell an interesting story, insert increasingly difficult challenges, see your character grow. . .

In some cases, like in the games known as "sandboxes", you don't win or lose, but you have fun anyways discovering and changing the world of the game in new ways.

In this game, in order to provide the illusion that the turtle moves to the right, we'll make the backdrop scroll to the left, with a technique known as scrolling. But, as you've learned, the backdrop can't move! To create the effect we want, therefore, we'll need to use a little trick: the backdrop will be composed by two Sprites that run one after one another for the entire duration of the game.

At the beginning of the game the first Sprite will coincide exactly with the Stage, and the second will be immediately to its right.

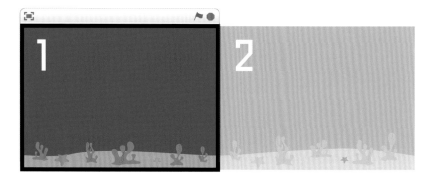

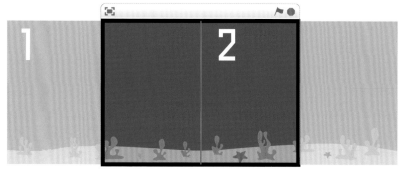

As soon as the space bar is pressed, the two sprites will start to glide to the left, at the same speed.

Every time that a Sprite will exit completely from the Stage area, it will reposition itself at the far right to start gliding again.

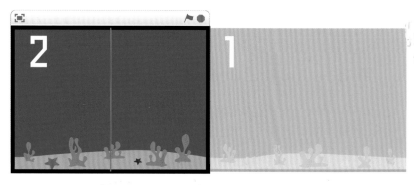

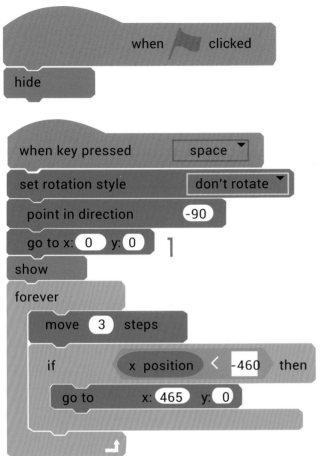

Our game will begin when the space bar is pressed. So only from that moment will the first Sprite simulating the backdrop have to appear and begin moving to the left.

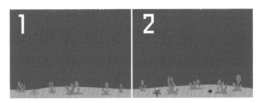

The two Sprites will have the same scripts except for the starting position:
in the first it is X: 0, Y: 0,
and in the second X: 465, Y: 0

When the green flag is clicked, there will be the main character on screen explaining the rules of the game. That means that the Sprite we've been working on will have to HIDE.

ce the space bar is clicked, it will turn to the left after we have blocked its ation style. At this point it can position itself at the center of the stage, that is X: 0, Y: 0, in order to cover it completely, and then to show itself. Now, to make it move, insert the block MOVE 3 STEPS inside a FOREVER.

In addition to moving, the Sprite will need to use an IF...THEN to check whether it has arrived at the end of the left part of the screen, that is whether it has gone past X: -460. At that point it will have to reposition itself back at the right, where its X is about 465.
If you have done everything correctly, now the second Sprite will be at the center of the stage, and the two Sprites will continue to move left and reposition themselves to the right forever.

JELLYFISH: MOVEMENT

The main character in the game will have to eat the jellyfish that, carried by the current, arrive near him.

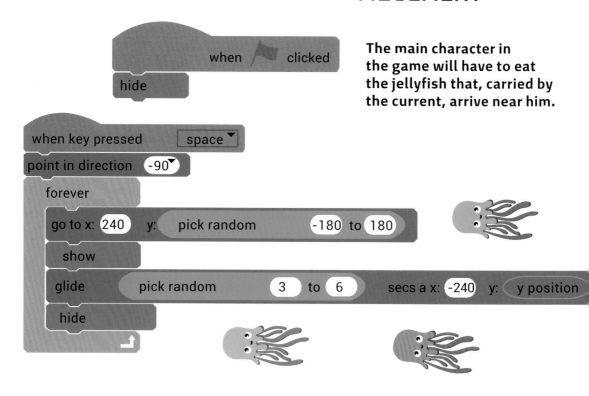

This script will be the same for all the jellyfish.

First of all, we have to change the Sprite's rotation style to RIGHT-LEFT, like you learned to do in Chapter 2, so they don't tip over! The jellyfish, like most of the elements in this game, will also have to stay hidden until the space bar is pressed.

At this point they will have to be turned left, and appear at a random point on the right edge of the Stage and glide to the left until they reach the end of the Stage. At that point, they'll have to hide.

But you've already programmed a similar movement for the project "Everybody to the Seaside", remember?

To make the jellyfish move at different speeds replace the seconds in the command GLIDE with the block PICK RANDOM 3 TO 6.

JELLYFISH: AMOUNTS FOR THE RECIPE

In order to check whether the turtle has eaten all the jellyfish necessary to win, we have to keep track of them!

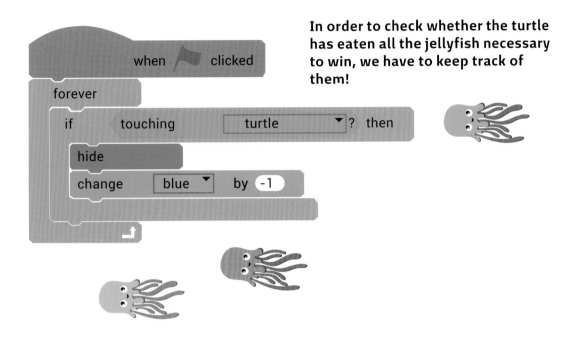

Create three variables, one for each jellyfish, and name them after the three colors of the jellyfish so you don't get confused.
They have to be valid variables for all the Sprites.
After that create a Script for each jellyfish to check whether it is TOUCHING the Sprite of the turtle, in which case it has to hide and change its variable by -1.

Make sure that each jellyfish changes only its own counter,
and not another's: so the blue jellyfish will change the variable "blue" by -1,
the yellow jellyfish the "yellow" variable, and the same for the red ones.

MIX THE INGREDIENTS

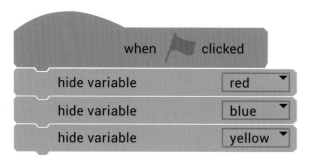

To make things more interesting, every time the game begins, it will select a different number of each color of jellyfish to be caught. Since this is not the job of one Sprite in particular, it will be the Stage that does it.

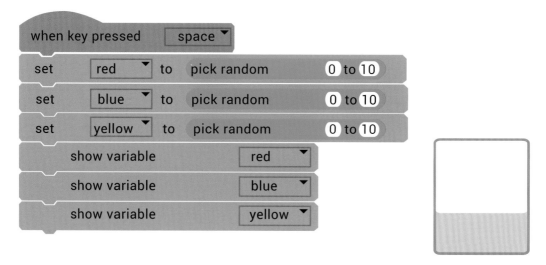

When the green flag is clicked, the three variables that you've just created must stay hidden. They must show themselves when the space bar is clicked, but first they have to know what value to take on! Insert the block PICK. . . RANDOM NUMBER 0 TO 10 for each jellyfish counter.

Winning and Losing

Now, always in the Script area of the Stage, let's check when it's time to end the game.

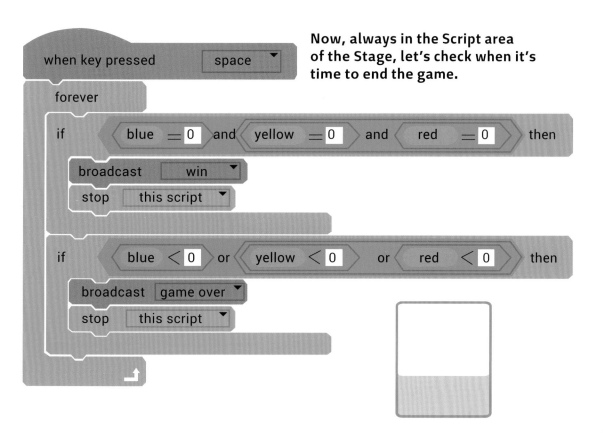

This is the Script where we'll define the conditions of winning and losing.

The Stage will broadcast the message "You Win" when all the jellyfish counters have reached 0.

If however even one of them is less than 0 because we have taken more jellyfish than needed, we'll lose the game and receive the "Game Over" message.

LET'S EAT!

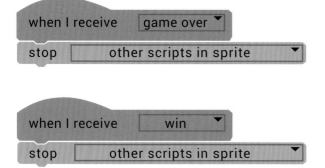

When they receive the messages that the game is over, nearly all the Sprites present on the scene will need to stop all of their scripts.

The Sprites of the turtle, the jellyfish, and the backdrop all have to stop running their scripts when the game ends. This way they will stop where they are and it won't be possible to move them anymore.

```
when  [flag]  clicked
say   HEY DUDE! HELP ME CATCH:                      for  2  secs
say   join   blue    and   blue jellyfishes,        for  2  secs
say   join   yellow  and   yellow,                  for  2  secs
say   join   rosso   e     red!!!!!                  for  2  secs
say   No more and no less                           for  2  secs
say   Press space when you are ready                for  2  secs
wait until   key [ space  ▼ ] pressed?
```

**Now's the time for our protagonist to take the stage.
He will be the one that explains the rules of the game to
use when all the other Sprites on the Stage will be hidden.
Then, once the space bar has been pressed, he'll be able
to move up and down using the arrow keys. There's no
need for him to move left and right, since the backdrop
will the one moving!**

When the green flag is clicked the turtle will have to tell us how many jellyfish
to catch of each color, then he'll wait for the space bar to be pressed. In the
previous script you have saved in the 3 variables "blue", "yellow", and "red"
random numbers from 0 to 10, so to make him tell us what numbers they are all
we need to do is insert each variable in a SAY block. But we don't want the turtle
to tell us only the number, he also has to tell us what it represents.
At any moment, if in a block we have one space and we need two spaces,
we can put in that space the operator JOIN. . . , like we have done here.

You have already learned how to move your characters with the arrows, just
remember to put WAIT UNTIL KEY SPACE PRESSED as the starting Event,
and to place the Sprite at the left of the Stage with a GO TO X: -160, Y: 0 block,
right after the starting Event.

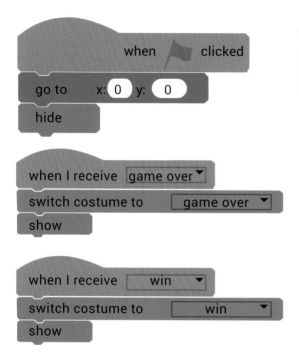

To signal if the player has won or lost we will use a Sprite in written form, with two costumes.

Place it at the center of the Stage at the beginning of the game and make it hide.

According to the message it receives it will change its costume.

Then the words "You Win!" will appear when the game ends in victory and "Game Over" if it ends in defeat.

WHAT WE'VE LEARNED:

- To set up a new project
- To program a random movement
- To change Sprites' costumes

- Interaction between the character and the environment
- To make Sprites talk

- Interaction between characters
- Random movement

- To manage the score of a game with variables
- To create new Events, with messages

- Clones: to create, manage, and delete them

- To program a game with horizontal scrolling
- To make sure that goal of the game changes each time to create an experience that is always different

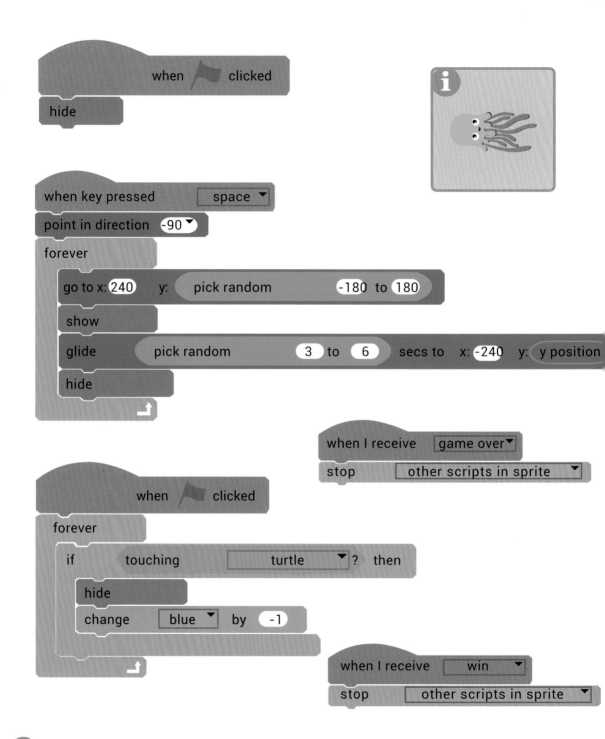

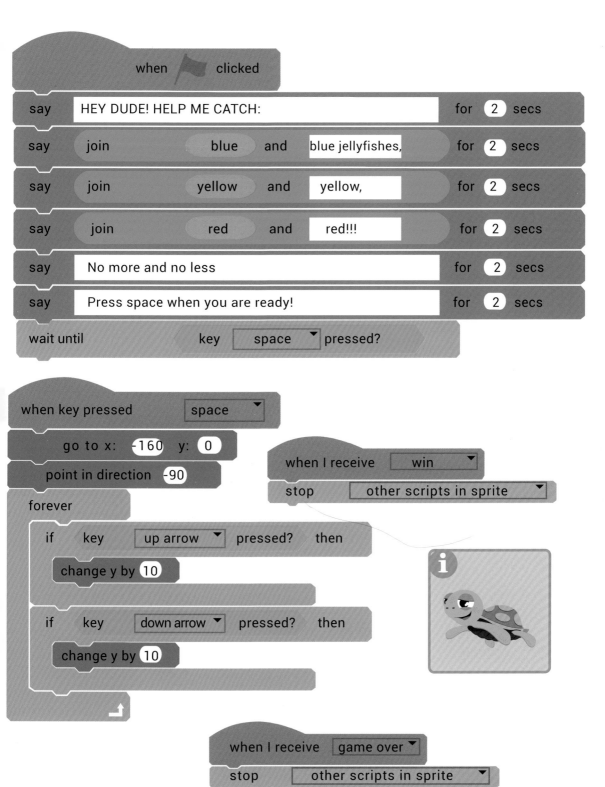

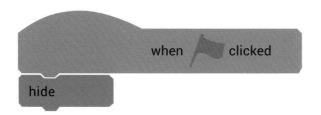

when 🚩 clicked

hide

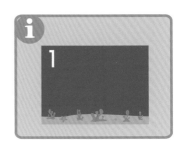

1

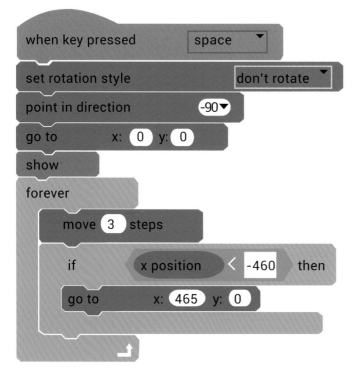

when key pressed   space ▼

set rotation style   don't rotate ▼

point in direction   -90 ▼

go to   x: 0 y: 0

show

forever

move 3 steps

if   x position < -460 then

go to   x: 465 y: 0

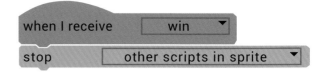

when I receive   win ▼

stop   other scripts in sprite ▼

when I receive   game over ▼

stop   other scripts in sprite ▼

when ⚑ clicked
hide

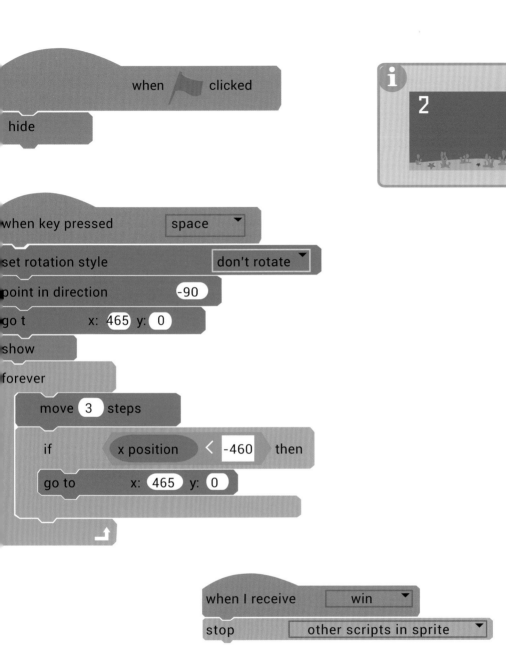

when key pressed [space ▼]
set rotation style [don't rotate ▼]
point in direction (-90)
go t   x: (465) y: (0)
show
forever
    move (3) steps
    if (x position < -460) then
        go to   x: (465) y: (0)

when I receive [win ▼]
stop [other scripts in sprite ▼]

when I receive [game over ▼]
stop [other scripts in sprite ▼]

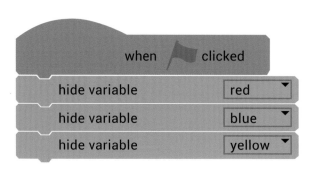

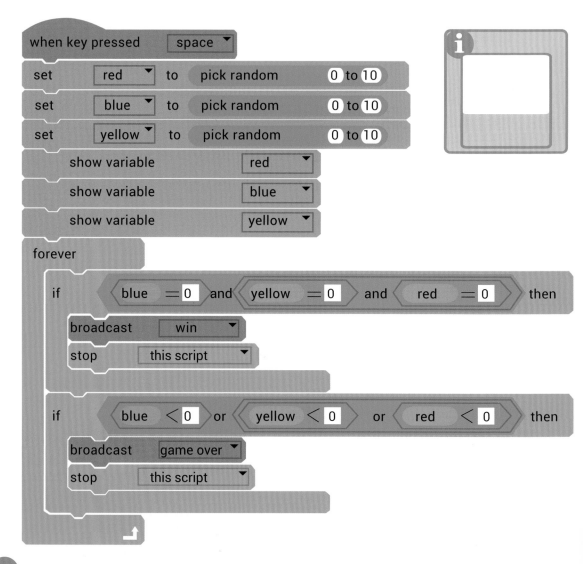

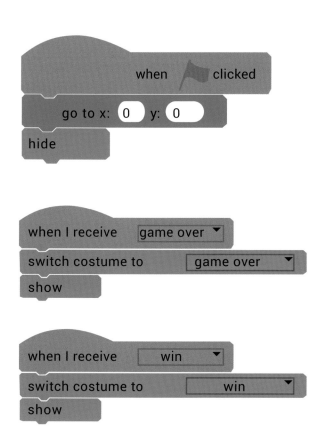

GET READY FOR THE NEXT CHALLENGE!

CHALLENGE

KRAKEN!

**It's easy to feast on jellyfish
when nobody is bothering you. . .**

Add an enemy to make the game
more difficult.
Insert the Squid Sprite
and tell it to move
to the left at random moments.

A hint:

Come on,
you're an expert now!

SOLUTIONS

DRAW YOUR OWN RACETRACK

In the New Backdrop section, click on the brush icon to draw. On the left you'll find all the tools you need to create your backdrop: try to fill it all with a single color with the PAINT BUCKET, and then to create your track with the ERASER.

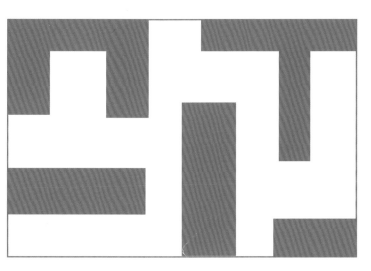

Or make an intricate labyrinth with help from the RECTANGLE TOOL or the LINE TOOL.

ROLE REVERSAL

First move the scripts of the Spaceship to the Alien, and vice versa.
This way you'll control the spaceship with the 4 arrow keys, while Zeno
will move randomly around the screen.
Now swap the blocks IF TOUCHING so as to assign the right behavior
to the two characters.

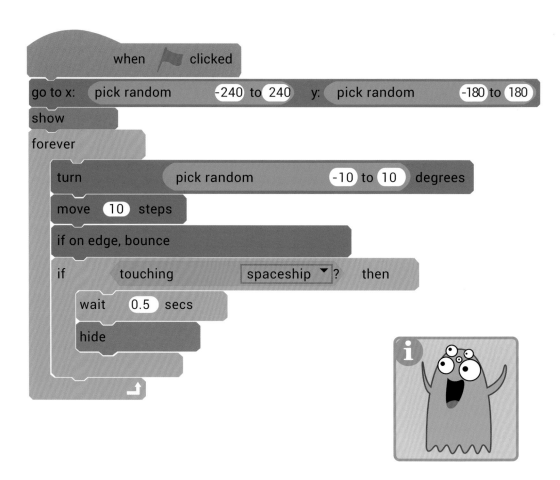

```
when 🏴 clicked
go to x: pick random  -240 to 240  y: pick random  -180 to 180
show
forever
    if  key  up arrow ▾ pressed?  then
        point in direction  0 ▾
        move 10 steps

    if  key  down arrow ▾ pressed?  then
        point in direction  180 ▾
        move 10 steps

    if  key  right arrow ▾ pressed?  then
        point in direction  90 ▾
        move 10 steps

    if  key  left arrow ▾ pressed?  then
        point in direction  -90 ▾
        move 10 steps

    if  touching  alien ▾ ?  then
        wait  1 secs
        glide  1 secs to  x: 0 y: 180
        hide
```

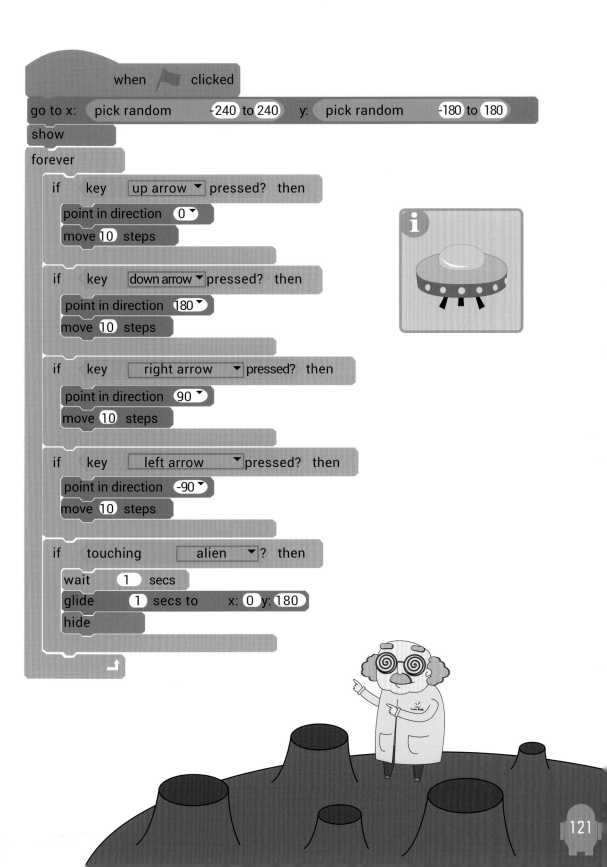

MILO SPEAKS!

Make Milo explain the rules of the game by using the block SAY...FOR...
SECONDS. At the end of the explanation make it so the game waits for
the space bar to be pressed in order to start. When it is pressed, the game
can begin: send a message, calling it "start": now edit the game so that
Milo starts moving and the objects start falling only when they receive
the message.

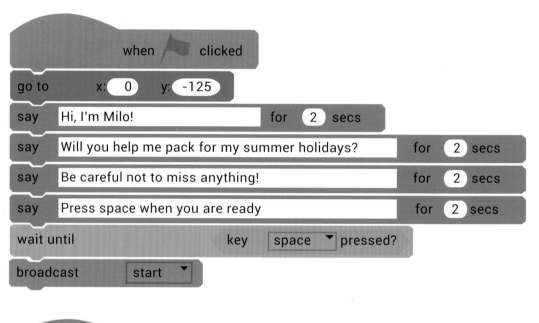

when 🏴 clicked

go to x: 0 y: -125

say Hi, I'm Milo! for 2 secs

say Will you help me pack for my summer holidays? for 2 secs

say Be careful not to miss anything! for 2 secs

say Press space when you are ready for 2 secs

wait until key space pressed?

broadcast start

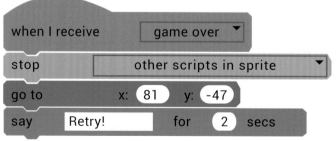

when I receive game over

stop other scripts in sprite

go to x: 81 y: -47

say Retry! for 2 secs

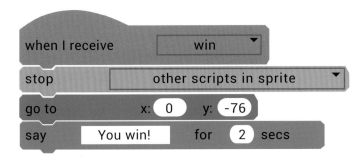

```
when I receive        win  ▼

stop            other scripts in sprite  ▼

go to         x: 0      y: -76

say      You win!       for   2   secs
```

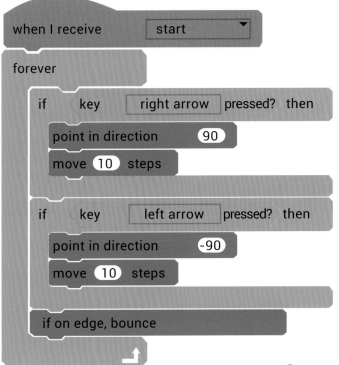

```
when I receive        start  ▼

forever

    if      key      right arrow   pressed?  then

        point in direction      90

        move  10  steps

    if      key      left arrow   pressed?  then

        point in direction      -90

        move  10  steps

    if on edge, bounce
```

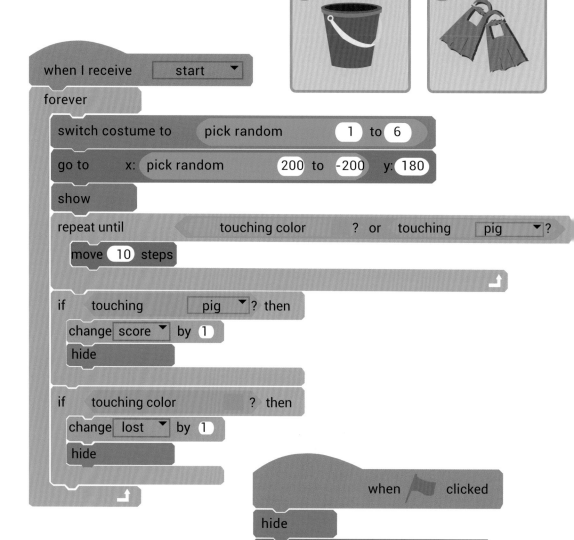

IT'S POURING RAIN!

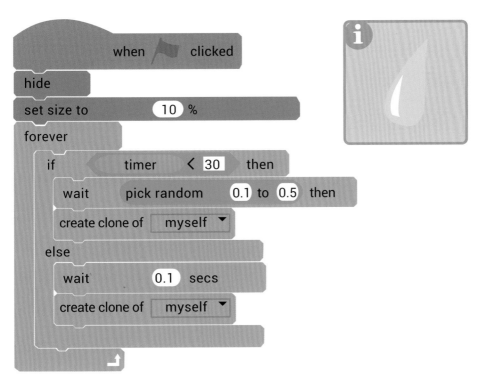

```
when [flag] clicked
hide
set size to (10) %
forever
    if < timer < [30] > then
        wait < pick random (0.1) to (0.5) > then
        create clone of [myself ▼]
    else
        wait (0.1) secs
        create clone of [myself ▼]
```

Start with a block of IF...THEN...ELSE. Build it so that IF fewer than 30 seconds have passed since the beginning of the game (timer < 30), the raindrop has to wait, before cloning itself, a random number from 0.1 to 0.5 seconds. Otherwise, if the timer has passed 30 seconds, it will wait only 0.1 seconds. This way the rain will fall much harder in the second half of the game.

KRAKEN!

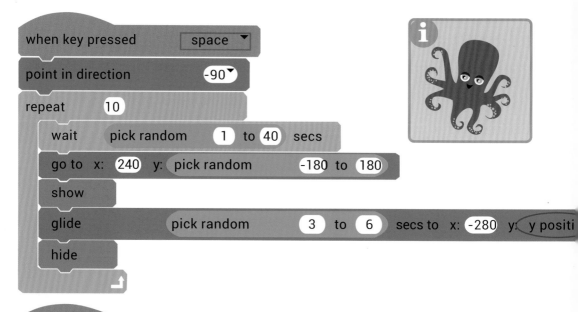

```
when key pressed    space ▼
point in direction    -90▼
repeat    10
    wait    pick random    1 to 40    secs
    go to x: 240 y: pick random    -180 to 180
    show
    glide    pick random    3 to 6    secs to x: -280 y: y positi
    hide
```

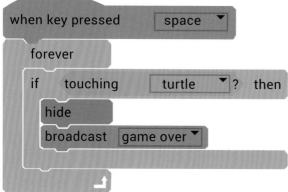

```
when key pressed    space ▼
    forever
    if    touching    turtle ▼ ? then
        hide
        broadcast    game over ▼
```

Add the squid as a new Sprite. At the signal to start the game (pressing the space bar) the squid has to follow the movement commands for a limited number of times (for example 10).

You'll notice that the Script is similar to the one that controls the movement of the jellyfish: the squid waits a random number of seconds - which can even be a long time to make him more unpredictable – then appears and moves horizontally to the left edge of the screen. At the same time, an IF. . . THEN block will cause the game to end when the squid touches the turtle.

DID YOU HAVE FUN? DO YOU WANT TO GO ON?
KEEP EXPERIMENTING WITH WHAT YOU HAVE
LEARNED BY CREATING NEW GAMES.

REMEMBER THAT SCRATCH IS ALSO A COMMUNITY!
ON THE WEBSITE YOU CAN FIND NEW PROJECTS
AND SHARE THE ONES YOU MAKE.

IF YOU WANT TO TEST YOURSELF WITH RIDDLES
AND ANIMATED STORIES, LOOK FOR OUR SECOND
BOOK.

CODING FOR KIDS.
CREATE YOUR OWN ANIMATED STORIES
WITH SCRATCH

These projects are the result of the experience
with the courses and workshops that Coder Kids
(www.coderkids. it) has organized and held in schools
both as an addition to the teaching curriculum and as
an extracurricular activity.

We take the opportunity to thank the children, their
families, and their teachers, for having participated with
such great enthusiasm and for being a continuous source
of inspiration to us.

CODER KIDS

Coder Kids (www.coderkids.it) has been organizing courses of computer programming and robotics for children and teens since 2014. The courses are done both in schools, as an addition to the teaching curriculum, and as an extracurricular activity.
The projects in this book, designed and created by Viviana Figus, Federico Vagliasindi, Federica Gambel and Johan Aludden, are the products of these laboratories.
For White Star Kids Coder Kids also published "Coding for Kids. Create your own Animated Stories with Scratch".

ILLUSTRATIONS
AND GRAPHIC DESIGN BY:

VALENTINA FIGUS

White Star Kids® is a registered trademark property of White Star s.r.l.

© 2017 White Star s.r.l.
Piazzale Luigi Cadorna, 6 - 20123 Milan, Italy
www.whitestar.it

Translation and editing: Iceigeo, Milan (Joshua Burkholder)

ISBN 978-88-544-1188-3
2 3 4 5 6   21 20 19 18 17

Printed in Italy by Rotolito Lombarda
Seggiano di Pioltello (MI)